Rules for the Dance

Other Books by Mary Oliver

POETRY

No Voyage and Other Poems
The River Styx, Ohio, and Other Poems
Twelve Moons
American Primitive
Dream Work
House of Light
New and Selected Poems
White Pine
West Wind

CHAPBOOKS

The Night Traveler
Sleeping in the Forest

PROSE

A Poetry Handbook
Blue Pastures

Rules for the Dance

A Handbook for Writing and Reading Metrical Verse

Mary Oliver

HarperCollins*Publishers*

ecco

An Imprint of HarperCollins Publishers, registered
in the United States of America and/or other jurisdictions.

www.harpercollins.com

Library of Congress Cataloging-in-Publication Data

Oliver, Mary, date.

Rules for the dance : a handbook for writing and reading

metrical verse / Mary Oliver.

p.   cm.

"A Mariner original."

ISBN 0-395-85086-x

ISBN 978-0-395-85086-2

1. English language — Versification. 2. English poetry — History
and criticism — Theory, etc. 3. Poetry — Authorship. I. Title.

PE1505.037   1998

821.009 – dc2   98-2625   CIP

Printed in the United States of America

23 24 25 26 27 LBC 32 31 30 29 28

Permissions acknowledgments begin on page 189

For Molly Malone Cook

True ease in writing comes from art, not chance,
As those move easiest who have learned to dance.

Alexander Pope, *"An Essay on Criticism"*

Foreword

I HAD THREE REASONS for writing this book on metrical poetry.

The first was to create for myself the opportunity to think about metrical prosody, which is an endlessly fertile subject for any working poet. By "working poet" I include those who write the modern non-rhyming, non-metrical form of lyric (which includes myself) — for the foundation of every poem is not only its words but its formality of motion, whether it be metrical altogether, or only at the occasional rhapsodic moment. Which is to say that I believe all poems are metrical to some extent, though they follow no predetermined pattern — but more of that later.

My second purpose was to develop an informational and thoughtful text giving the basic rules of scansion, along with a collection of metrical poems for immediate example and pleasure, to writers who actually want to write metrical verse.

My third purpose — and this is by no means the least of the three — was to offer to readers of poetry a text and a commentary which would help them understand the metrical process:

that is, not only how the metrical poem should be written, but how it should be read, or received, by the reader. On every page that follows, I consider the reader equal in importance to the writer, if not more important.

Metrical poetry belongs to a certain era — a few centuries — and with every passing year that contained time grows more distant, its methods more estranged from our own. The reader of modern poetry feels at ease with the cadences of conversation. To read Chaucer's poems, now, requires a diligent and even extraordinary effort; it requires, indeed, a specialized knowledge of the language and the versification of Chaucer's time. The same thing, in our age, is happening to metrical poetry. It is no longer a safe bet that students will have been prepared for meter by having heard, over and over, the rhythms of Mother Goose. In schools, students are urged to follow their own unpatterned expressions, and little if any memorization of metrical poems is now required.

As a result, students and other readers of Milton, of Shakespeare, of Wordsworth, of Wilfred Owen, even of Frost, come to the poems, frankly, with tin ears. They cannot scan. They don't know an iamb from an anapest. They read for comprehension and hear little if anything of the interwoven pleasures of the sound and the pattern of the poem, which are also deeply instructive concerning the statement of the poem, along with the meanings of the words themselves. Not knowing how to listen, they read the poem but they do not hear it sing, or slide, or slow down, or crush with the heel of sound, or leap off the line, or hurry, or sob, or refuse to move from the self-pride of the calm pentameter no matter what fire is rustling through it.

Every poem is a statement.

Every poem is music — a determined, persuasive, reliable, enthusiastic, and crafted music.

Without an understanding of this music, Shakespeare is only the sense we can make of him; he is the wisdom without the shapeliness, which is one half of the poem.

So, most of all, I wrote this book to help readers of metrical poems enter the thudding deeps and the rippling shallows of sound-pleasure and rhythm-pleasure. I hope their understanding and pleasure of metric poetry will be deepened and complicated, so much so that their response to the poems becomes not only comprehension, but comprehension accompanied by a felt experience.

Why is it important for students — for any of us, in fact — to have this experience?

Poems speak of the mortal condition; in poems we muse (as we say) about the tragic and glorious issues of our fragile and brief lives: our passions, our dreams, our failures. Our wonderings about heaven and hell — these too are in poems. Life, death; mystery, and meaning. Five hundred years and more of such labor, such choice thought within choice expression, lies within the realm of metrical poetry. Without it, one is uneducated, and one is mentally poor.

Following the text is a small anthology of metrical poems. These I selected primarily as useful illustrations. I am sorry it was not practical to include more. But the world is amazingly full of books. They are everywhere! The great poems are easy to find, rare and priceless though they be.

*

Finally, I am aware that there are among the poems very few by women. It is a fact, though a sad one, that poets of the past few centuries, at least published poets, were almost all men. I wish it had not been so. It is, of course, a denial and a closure that need never happen again.

Contents

PART ONE: THE RULES

1. Breath *3*

2. Patterns *6*

3. More About Patterns *19*

4. Design: Line Length *29*

5. Release of Energy Along the Line *36*

6. Design: Rhyme *40*

7. Design: Traditional Forms *50*

8. Words on a String *57*

9. Mutes and Other Sounds *60*

10. The Use of Meter in Non-Metric Verse *62*

11. The *Ohs* and the *Ahs* *65*

12. Image-Making *67*

PART TWO: THE DANCERS ONE BY ONE

13. Style *79*

PART THREE: SCANSION, AND THE ACTUAL WORK

14. Scansion: Reading the Metrical Poem *87*

15. Scansion: Writing the Metrical Poem *90*

16. Yourself Dancing: The Actual Work *93*

PART FOUR: A UNIVERSAL MUSIC

17. Then and Now *103*

Envoi 104

PART FIVE: AN ANTHOLOGY OF METRICAL POEMS
109

Permissions *189*

Index *190*

Rules for the Dance

Part One
The Rules

1

Breath

METRICAL POETRY is about: breath. Breath as an intake and a flow. Breath as a pattern. Breath as an indicator, perhaps the most vital one, of mood. Breath as our own personal tie with all the rhythms of the natural world, of which we are a part, from which we can never break apart while we live. Breath as our first language.

A cardinal attribute of breath (or breathing) is, of course, its repetition. The galloping footbeats of the heart, that spell fear. Or the slow and relaxed stretch of breath of the sleeping child. In either case, by their repetition, they make a pattern. Truly this pattern is as good as a language.* It reveals a great deal: the depth of sleep, the stress or the ease of the breather. If the pattern changes, we know it reflects something important — mood has plunged, or health has been touched by crisis, or the inner life, without being seen externally, has pressed upon the heart, has tightened or loosened the lungs. *It is as good as a language.* We sigh. We pant. We reveal ourselves.

All of this just said about breathing pertains also to the

---

*Think of EKG and EEG, wave patterns which offer such personal and accurate information about our bodies, and which physicians "read."

design of the metrical poem, which is composed of rhyme, and line length, and a metrical pattern in a construct of repetition.

In *West-Running Brook,* Robert Frost included a poem called "Bereft"; it isn't hard to gather the evidence for its title from the text — to read the poem, that is, for comprehension. To read it in silence. But what is this poem without the unchanging rave of its pattern, its attempts to get out of the place it is stuck in? It is not the poem Frost made; it is not the poem that he would have us hear.

Bereft

Where had I heard this wind before
Change like this to a deeper roar?
What would it take my standing there for,
Holding open a restive door,
Looking down hill to a frothy shore?
Summer was past and day was past.
Somber clouds in the west were massed.
Out in the porch's sagging floor,
Leaves got up in a coil and hissed,
Blindly struck at my knee and missed.
Something sinister in the tone
Told me my secret must be known:
Word I was in the house alone
Somehow must have gotten abroad,
Word I was in my life alone,
Word I had no one left but God.

The poem is only sixteen lines long. It doesn't take a lot of time, therefore, to explain what it is saying. Anyway, design says it better. We begin by reading it, as we would any poem, using natural expression and common sense. Immediately we feel that each line is built to be struck, heavily, four times (as indicated here by accents). The length of each line gives us a slight edginess; there is in it something uncomfortable, some vague stricture. Rhyme usually changes, easily and often; the poem throws out a sound, and then its match, and then moves on. But not here. Here the same rhyme persists through five lines, until it feels like what it is: a stagnation, an inability to move forward. It feels like the dreadful unsolvable weight of human woe.

And the heavy stress at the end of each line somehow makes of the silence after the line a precipitous and dangerous fall. And somehow the heavy stress at the beginning of each line bespeaks a degree of anguish: it is such a clumsy entrance, the entrance of a speaker so pinched and desperate he lacks all ease, all ability simply to step into the line — he has to grab hold or fall.

Everything here, in other words, is meaningful: the left and right edges, the shape of the poem, the inexorable repetition, the rhyming pattern and the dolorous rhymes themselves. The change at the end of the poem from the rhyme "known"/"alone" to the final one, "abroad"/"God," is significantly slight, inching toward a finality as other rhymes in other poems might well jump to a significantly "new" rhyming sound, at some point of discovery. Here there is no such jump, only a holding on.

Read in this way, the poem begins to exist not only literally, and intellectually, but palpably.

Said Frost, "For my part I should be as satisfied to play tennis with the net down as to write verse with no verse form set to stay me."

Okay.

But how did he do it?

2

Patterns

UNDERLYING THE CONSTRUCT of the metrical poem is the certainty that all sound and all patterns, as well as words, are sensible to interpretation.

To begin, then, at the beginning. The metrical poem is a pattern made with sound just as much as it is a statement made through sound.

The rules by which this pattern is constructed are as certain and ongoing, though not so irreplaceably or so strictly kept, as are the rules of linear measurement — inches, feet, yards, rods, etc. They are less rigid because the metrical pattern of a poem is an apparatus meant to illuminate feeling and meaning, rather than a declaration of fact as an end in itself, the way nine inches means nine inches, unvaryingly. Also, the allowable leniency offers room for individuality — that is, style. And, finally, the successful conveyance of meaning can, sometimes, require a procedure different from the expected.

Metrical poems have three components which, taken together, compose the overall scheme. The first is *rhyme*, the second is *line length*, and the third is the metrical *pattern* used.

Even as the ruler needs inches to keep things regular, the metrical line needs some unit of division to keep things in order. Every line of a metrical poem is divided into a certain number of *feet*. Each foot contains one complete unit of some metrical *pattern*.

Where had	I heard	this wind	before
Foot 1	*Foot 2*	*Foot 3*	*Foot 4*

There are many such patterns. In this handbook we will attend to the four most common, whose names are *iambic, trochaic, dactylic,* and *anapestic.*

The process of their construction is not unlike the division of music into units called measures or bars — units that contain both a repetition of rhythm and, if the composer wishes, a certain allowable amount and kind of variation upon that rhythm.

In the metrical poem as in music, such varieties and variations do not violate the established pattern, but give it added excitement and interest. They are the gestures and flourishes that compound the ongoing drama of sound, the sound of the music or the poem: steady beat *and* counterpoint.

It is fair to say that the metrical poem has a quality that is unbreakably and reliably musical.

Here are the opening lines of a metrical poem:

> Loveliest of trees, the cherry now
> Is hung with bloom along the bough,
> And stands about the woodland ride
> Wearing white for Eastertide.
>
> (A. E. Housman, "Loveliest of Trees")

And here are four lines (a complete poem) which are not metrical:

> O my songs,
> Why do you look so eagerly and so curiously into
>   people's faces,
> Will you find your lost dead among them?
>
> (Ezra Pound, "Coda")

In the four-line metrical stanza, the arrangement of the words strives to elicit a rhythm of alternating stresses, light then heavy, light then heavy. Though the rhythm is touched with a difference or two (the initial syllables of both the first and the fourth lines pull in a different direction), there is a definite, ongoing *pattern* which the reader is meant to hear. In Pound's short poem, the cadences are those of natural speech. The poem is wonderful, but it is not patterned. It has no rhythm which we can grasp, and which we easily begin to anticipate as we read through the lines.

Rhythm is made up of the continual tonal rise and fall of speech, by writing the words down in such a way that the inflections, heavy or light, will fall at certain points only, or mainly, to make a pattern, as in the Housman example. Inflection helps to release the meaning of language. Indeed, there is no satisfactory language without it. In metrical poetry, it is the basis of everything; it is the reason why there can be a pattern.

If words, with their few or many syllables, are the material of language, inflection surely is its spirit. Almost all words of more than one syllable contain at least one syllable which is uttered with special emphasis, and others which are spoken lightly. As in "twenty," or "people," or the word "emphasis" itself.

In addition to such variation within a word, there is meaningful and necessary inflection within the phrasing of any group of words. Many words in the English language have only one syllable, and still inflection — both in the metrical poem and in ordinary speech — must be created to release the meaning of what is said. The specifics of inflection create tone; tone shapes meaning.*

It would seem likely that emphasis would fall for this purpose upon verbs and nouns, the important parts of speech, rather than upon the less important connectives, articles, or prepositions. And in the flow of ordinary speech this is, sensibly, true. "<u>Hurry</u>, I see a <u>bluebird</u>, it's on your <u>mailbox</u>!" you call to someone, and it is the underlined words that you emphasize.

In the metrical poem there is less certainty about the words that are to be spoken with emphasis, since there are in the metrical poem, always, two forces at work: *sense* and *pattern.* The emphasis can, and often will, point to important parts of the syntax, as in the following line:

The <u>dew</u> was <u>gone</u> that <u>made</u> his <u>blade</u> so <u>keen</u>. . . .

(Robert Frost, "The Tuft of Flowers")

Yet there may also be lines in which the force of the pattern rules. Thus the same poem has lines like the following:

I <u>thought</u> of <u>questions</u> <u>that</u> have <u>no</u> reply,

or

---

*If inflection is absent, the impression given is of something mechanical, even sinister. Someone enters a bank, waves a gun, and says in an uninflected tone, *"Don't move!"* Mostly, we speak to be heard and, when heard, to be answered. Language is essentially a dialogue. But not in this case.

The mower in the dew had loved them thus,

in which the rather minor words "that" and "in" are spoken with an emphasis. Such emphasis does not cross meaning, for meaning is paramount of course. But the metrical poem is, without question, very forcibly pattern-driven.

Scansion is the mechanical notation of the metrical pattern of a poem; in this process every syllable of every word is accounted for, and both the prevailing pattern and all variations are revealed.

In order to write and to read metrical poems, an understanding of scansion is essential. In no other way can the process of metrics be explored, and comprehended both in its inflexible and its relaxable latitudes.

In the process of scansion, syllables to be given heavy stress are indicated by a stroke (´) placed at the end of the stressed syllable, and syllables to be given light stress are indicated by a curved mark (˘) placed directly over that syllable.* So, still using the initial Frost line, we have the following:

The dew was gone that made his blade so keen. . . .

Since we are looking at only one line here, and since rhyme is a matter of the relationship of sounds, we will put the subject of rhyme aside for the moment in order to concentrate on pattern, and the length of the line.

---

*The symbol placed over the light syllable is also known as the *breve,* and the symbol indicating a heavy syllable the *macron.*

Each line of the poem carries within it, repeated over and over, foot by foot, a rhythm, which creates the pattern, sometimes exactly and sometimes with some permissible variation. *Each foot is constructed of a single emphasis plus details* — that is, one heavy stress and no more, and whatever light stresses are needed to make up the chosen pattern.

Thus, by reading the line as naturally as possible, and counting the heavy stresses, one can find* the number of feet in the line. *The pattern of the poem does not intend to be obscure but to be discernible through sensible reading.*

In the line given here, it is easy counting: there are five heavy stresses and five light stresses. The line has five feet.

> The dew was gone that made his blade so keen. . . .

If the line had read

> And the dew was gone that made his blade so heavy . . .

it would still be a five-foot line, since we are finding the answer by counting only the heavy stresses. Similarly, this line

> A thing of beauty is a joy for ever:

also, since it has five heavy stresses, is a five-foot line. And this one,

> Under the wide and starry sky . . .

---

*Almost always. This chapter on the general rules will be closely followed by a discussion of exceptions.

which, when we read it naturally, has four heavy stresses, is surely a four-foot line; and the following

> Likĕ ă Poĕt hídden
> Ín thĕ lighť oϝ thoughť,

are certainly three-foot lines.

The proper names of such lines, according to their length, are given in the following chart.

Names of Metrical Lines According to Length

A one-foot line is called monometer.

A two-foot line is called dimeter.

A three-foot line is called trimeter.

A four-foot line is called tetrameter.

A five-foot line is called pentameter.

A six-foot line is called hexameter.

A seven-foot line is called heptameter.

An eight-foot line is called octameter.

So we can say that the original line we are using for illustration, with its five heavy stresses, is a pentameter line. Now we turn our attention to the individual metric feet within the line.

The next chart indicates the four primary meters — the four metrical patterns — which we will be discussing. Later on you will quickly recognize each of them by its distinctive music. But to begin you need to memorize all four — their names, patterns, and notations.

Metrical Patterns and Their Symbols

Iamb: a light stress followed by a heavy stress. ˘ ´

Trochee: a heavy stress followed by a light stress. ´ ˘

Dactyl: a heavy stress followed by two light stresses. ´ ˘ ˘

Anapest: two light stresses followed by a heavy stress. ˘ ˘ ´

Using this chart, we see that the Frost line is a series of *iambs* repeated five times — five times we get a combination of a light stress followed by a heavy stress. And by adding vertical strokes to indicate the separate feet, we can scan the line to completion and perfection, as follows:

The dew | was gone | that made | his blade | so keen . . .

and we can properly and correctly name it an *iambic pentameter* line.

Every metrical poem is composed of an ongoing single pattern, which prevails throughout the poem. But it is not, frequently is not, the only meter employed. Substitutions are allowed; variation is not only sometimes necessary because of the syllable pattern of some word, it may well be in itself enhancing. Change within the pattern may occur for inflection, for expression, for emphasis, for nuance, for common sense, and because a rhythm without some variation within it is a dull rhythm.

Any one of the four patterns given may at any time be substituted for any other.

The question of how much substitution is allowed is unanswerable. Nothing is certain but success — if substitution is used too much, the pleasing sense of a pattern will be lost, at which point all is lost. If no substitution is used, the poem may take on a doggerel quality, and a feeling that complexity has been sacrificed for regularity.

As you see in the chart, the *trochee* (or *trochaic* foot) reverses the iambic — the heavy stress falls first, followed by a single light stress. The trochee is endlessly useful as a variant in an otherwise iambic line, as in the first line of "Bereft," or in the following:

> Something | there is | that does|n't love | a wall. . . .
>
> ("Mending Wall")

The forceful opening stress of the trochee is more dramatic than the invitational, in-stepping iambic. It is for this reason, I imagine, that Frost often uses it as the initial foot of a line when he begins with a proper name or place name:

> Silas | is what | he is — |we would|n't mind him —
>
> ("The Death of the Hired Man")

> Mother | can make | a com|mon ta|ble rear
> And kick | with two | legs like | an ar|my mule. . . .
>
> ("The Witch of Coös")

In each of these examples the proper name is naturally a trochee — yet Frost, who built the lines, could have placed such words within the line had he wanted to, and as he sometimes did, stretching the word across two feet to avoid the trochaic effect:

Poŏr Sĭ|lăs, só | cŏncerneá | fŏr oth|ĕr folḱ. . . .

("The Death of the Hired Man")

When the line is altogether trochaic, the effect is formal, even artificial; certainly it is not natural. Iambic meter seems to carry upon its broad and unexcitable back the cadence of sensible speech, and it almost does — our natural speech flow has many iambic "units." Yet speech is instanced by a continual disruption of any sustained pattern.

Trochaic verse has no such similar-to-natural sound. It is altogether like something composed, for it *is* something composed. Longfellow's pleasant but truly acrobatic *The Song of Hiawatha* is written in trochaic lines, a repeated drumlike pattern:

And thĕ | daughtĕr | of Nŏ|kómĭs
Grew up | like thĕ | prairĭĕ | lilĭĕs,
Grew a | tall ănd | slendĕr | maidĕn,
With thĕ | beauty | of thĕ | moonliğht. . . .

A second and familiar instance of the trochaic occurs in *Macbeth*, as the witches howl their culinary song:

Doublĕ, | doublĕ | toil ănd | troublĕ;
Firĕ | burn ănd | cauldrŏn | bubblĕ. . . .

The *dactyl*, also, is a composed and formal foot. Natural-seeming enough in certain words (háppinĕss, lóvelĭnĕss), when used as a pattern it becomes a "music" almost deafening the sense of what is being said. Again, Longfellow, with his interest in New World subjects married to traditional forms, offers us an obvious example. His long poem *Evangeline* (written in dactyls with an occasional iambic or trochaic foot) begins:

> Thĭs ĭs thĕ | fórĕst prĭ|mévăl. Thĕ | múrmŭrĭng | pínes
> ănd thĕ | hémlŏcks.
> Beárdĕd wĭth | mŏss, ănd ĭn | gármĕnts | green,
>   ĭndĭs|tínct ĭn thĕ | twílĭght,
> Stánd lĭke | Drúĭds ŏf | eld. . . .

The dactyl, like the trochee, is a useful variant in the iambic line:

> Ĭ wándĕr'd lónelў ăs ă cloúd
> Thăt floáts ŏn hígh o'ĕr válĕs ănd hílls,
> Whĕn áll ăt óncĕ Ĭ sáw ă crowd,
> Ă hóst, ŏf góldĕn dáffŏdíls;
> Bĕsídĕ thĕ láke, bĕneáth thĕ treés,
> Flúttĕrĭng ănd dáncĭng ín thĕ breezé.*

(Wordsworth, "I Wander'd Lonely . . .")

The *anapest*, the fourth metrical pattern, is the reverse of the dactyl — two light stresses are followed by a heavy stress. It too is

---

*Of course many words may be pronounced correctly in more than one way — say, with three syllables or with two, as is true of the word "fluttering." Here,

a composed and formal and altogether uncommon prevailing meter, though the anapest foot itself, light-footed and full of energy, is necessary on occasion and always full of wonderful uplift:

> The world is too much with us; late and soon,
> Getting and spending, we lay waste our powers:
> Little we see in Nature that is ours;
> We have given our hearts away, a sordid boon!
>
> (Wordsworth, "The World Is Too Much With Us . . .")

And here are some lines from Lord Byron's galloping poem "The Destruction of Sennacherib," altogether anapestic:

> The Assyrian came down like a wolf on the fold,
> And his cohorts were gleaming in purple and gold;
> And the sheen of their spears was like stars on the sea,
> When the blue wave rolls nightly on deep Galilee.

There is a fifth foot pattern — not properly a meter — which is used with fair frequency, the *spondee*. It is an accommodation for words that have no inflection although they have two syllables; examples are "heartbreak," "nightmare," "tomcat," and so forth. When such a word is used to create a foot, and the emphasis within the foot is therefore equally balanced, two horizontal lines, one over each of the two syllables, indicates the spondee:

heartbreak   nightmare

---

however, the three-syllable pronunciation surely creates an actual audible and palpable *fluttering*.

A spondee may also be indicated when the emphasis, within a single foot, is read as equal for two one-syllable words, as in the following:

Rōugh wīnds dŏ shaké thĕ dárlĭng budś ŏf Maý. . . .

(Shakespeare, Sonnet 18)

What one reader would read as an iamb, another might legitimately read as a spondee — scansion has rules but also elasticity, a willingness to coexist with a reasonable amount of individuality. Thus, in a line of Frost's previously quoted, the third foot can be read either as an iamb or as a spondee:

Ănd kićk wĭth twó lĕgs liké ăn ármў mulé . . .
Ănd kićk wĭth twó lĕgs līke ăn ármў mulé. . . .

("The Witch of Coös")

And here is another example, easily found (for they are many):

Gettĭng ănd spéndĭng, wé lăy wasté oŭr pówĕrs . . .
Gettĭng ănd spéndĭng, wé lăy wāste oŭr pówĕrs . . .

(Wordsworth, "The World Is Too Much With Us . . .")

The spondee, like the four metrical patterns, may be used freely as a substitute for any other prevailing meter.

3

More About Patterns

IAMBIC METER gives a graceful, motionful sense of balance
and unexcited progress. It is the most common meter in English
metrical poetry — one might even say that it is *the* meter of
English verse. Certainly it is the mainstay. All other meters offer
useful and necessary variety; also they are the means to vivid but
"unreal" acrobatics. Iambic meter, in comparison with the other
patterns, is the least obviously composed.

Shakespeare uses the iambic meter, in the pentameter line, in
both the plays and the sonnets:

> This above all: to thine own self be true,
> And it must follow, as the night the day
> Thou canst not then be false to any man.
>
> (*Hamlet*)

or

> A horse! a horse! my kingdom for a horse!
>
> (*Richard III*)

or

> When, in disgrace with Fortune and men's eyes,
> I all alone beweep my outcast state. . . .

(Sonnet 29)

And here is Wordsworth:

> The winds that will be howling at all hours,
> And are up-gather'd now like sleeping flowers;

and Keats:

> The poetry of earth is never dead . . .

and Marvell, on a shorter line:

> The grave's a fine and private place,
> But none, I think, do there embrace.

All of these lines, whatever their length, proceed steadily, without pause and without flourish. Their pace is a kind of neutral *flow*. There is enough pattern for the reader to feel the ongoing motion, yet this pattern is simple enough that contemplation can accompany its felt pressure.

Against the simple and the smooth, vivacity flashes the most brightly. So, when lines are not altogether iambic, but are engaged with variety, a nice disturbance is created and felt — a bounce, a flounce, a turn, a change — before the restoration of the original pattern takes place, which it does, usually, very quickly, an instance of pattern-drivenness. For example:

Ă sweet̆ dĭsórdĕr iń thĕ dress̆
Kińdlĕs iń clothĕs ă wańtŏnness̆.

(Robert Herrick, "Delight in Disorder")

We have seen this before, the change of an initial foot from the iambic to the trochaic, in an earlier discussion of a Frost line. Here I want to draw attention not only to the dramatic emphasis placed at the beginning of the line by the variation in the meter, but to the effect of the two light stresses which are thereby put together. Between "Kindles" and "clothes" there occurs, with this twinning of light stresses, a levitation, a leaping, an instant of nimble high-spiritedness, as the syllables arc between the two heavier strokes. It feels very different from the smooth riverbed of the regular iambic. This is a dancing part of the forward motion, the briefest yet most pleasant upward pitch of spirits, led by the pattern.

The same effect, a quick leaping, occurs when the trochee is used instead of the iamb anywhere along the line. The only place where it does not work reasonably is in the final foot, since the line is meant to feel like a unit, and by the end of the unit, for the feeling of completion, the original pattern (with its last heavy stress) pulls to be restored.

There is, in the previous Wordsworth quote, in the final foot of each line, an extra syllable which is given a light stress. This light stress is not, of course, a part of the iambic pattern. It is an accommodation to the words themselves ("hours" and "flowers"*), which end with a light stress. Such words have, we say, *feminine* endings, as opposed to "place," or "embrace," which are

---

*See note on page 16.

masculine. When such feminine words occur in the final foot of the line, they may be scanned as a *tag,* a light stress, which in the notation of scansion is not counted.

Thĕ windś	thăt wilĺ	bĕ howĺ	iñg át	aĺl hoúrs̆
Foot 1	*Foot 2*	*Foot 3*	*Foot 4*	*Foot 5 tag*

Now we come to an important and inevitable fact: that the meters are not always "regularly" employed. Twice now I have used the word "accommodation," and we are far from done. When the meter *is* totally regular, it is called *pure,* and when it is not, it is called *impure.* By "impure" I am not talking about variety of meter, or substitution of one meter for another, or even of the feminine tag, but of instances where, in one or more feet, there is a substantial alteration from the very specific recognizable pattern.

Here are two familiar lines:

> Hĭckŏry̆, dĭcḱŏry̆, docḱ;
> Thĕ mouś́e răn uṕ thĕ clocḱ.*

Line 2 is pure iambic, a trimeter line. Line 1, however, is not pure; it is composed of two dactyls and a final heavy stroke. It is, therefore, impure dactylic.

Such an abbreviation of the final foot is not uncommon.

---

*Grudgingly I admit that "hickory" and "dickory" could be elided into two-syllable words, trochees, and in fact this was brought to my attention by an observant editor who has seen at least one American edition so offering it: "Hick'ry, dick'ry." But I say: alas, what leaping in the mouth is thus lost.

THE RULES

Here are the two opening lines of another poem — this time the prevailing meter is trochaic — which utilizes the same device:

> Týgĕr! Týgĕr! búrnĭng bríght
> In thĕ fórĕsts ŏf thĕ níght. . . .

When such a truncation of the final foot occurs, the process is called *catalexis;* the foot itself is called *catalectic.* It is not regular. It is impure. But it is also perfectly proper! And, on occasion, wonderfully effective.

Consider how very different from the Blake lines are the feeling of some lines from Longfellow's *The Song of Hiawatha,* with its unceasing pure trochees, each final foot with a last light lifted syllable:

> Cán ĭt bé thĕ sún dĕscéndĭng,
> O'ér thĕ lévĕl pláin ŏf wátĕr?
> Ór thĕ Réd Swăn flóatĭng flýĭng,
> Wóundĕd bý thĕ mágĭc árrŏw. . . .

In the Blake poem, that final heavy stroke at the end of the line is one more hammer blow upon the forge of creation which is a major presence throughout the poem. The effect of the catalexis is, if you will, in tune with the subject of the Blake poem, as it clearly is not in tune with Longfellow's poem, in which each foot is an exact echo of the one preceding it.

Thus, such named accommodations as catalexis may more properly be thought of as extensions of the rules rather than oppositions to the rules.

*

Here are the names of more "irregularities":

When a foot within the line or at the beginning of the line lacks a syllable (it would have to be a light syllable, as there can be, properly, no foot without a heavy stress), it is called a *lame* foot. Here is an example from a poem by Edna St. Vincent Millay, called "Moriturus," a vigorous poem in sturdy dimeter:

> Ăwaré | ŏf thĕ flight
> Ŏf thĕ gŏl|dĕn flíckĕr
> Wĭth hĭs wing | tŏ thĕ light;
> Tŏ heár | hĭm níckĕr
>
> Ănd drúm | wĭth hĭs bíll
> Ŏn thĕ rót|tĕd wíllŏw;
> *Lame Foot* ⟶ Snúg | ănd stíll
> Ŏn ă grey | píllŏw
>
> Deép ĭn | thĕ claý
> Whĕre díg|gĭng ĭs hard,
> Oút ŏf | thĕ way, —
> The blué | shard ⟵ *Lame foot*
>
> Ŏf ă bró|kĕn pláttĕr —

Sometimes it is difficult to determine which foot in a line is the lame foot. Since there is always a prevailing pattern, and since the prevailing pattern here is iambic, the first foot of the line "Snug and still" is the lame foot — the initial light stress is absent. For the same reason, the second foot of the line "The blue shard" is the lame one; the first foot is an iamb in fine order, the second foot has only the heavy stress. (This is *not* catalexis, since the *final* stress of the iamb, properly speaking, is in place.)

Another example:

Ĭ knŏw | ă bank | where | the wild | thyme grows. . . .
↑ (Shakespeare, *A Midsummer Night's Dream*)

Here the third foot lacks any addition to the single heavy stress
— heavy beyond a doubt, since it is the only syllable in the foot.
How easy it would have been simply to say "whereon the wild
thyme grows," and have it not be lame. But then, how melodic
the line would have been — how without pause, without that
inner thoughtfulness we feel as Oberon slowly, craftily, considers
his next move. Even lame feet can be meaningful, and graceful.

Just as you might expect, there is also a name for a foot that
has within it too many stresses, to accommodate an overabun-
dance of syllables. Such a foot does not occur with any frequency,
yet often enough that it will be helpful to recognize it, and also of
course to know about it in order to use it if needed. The example
below comes again from Millay's "Moriturus," the final lines of
the poem.

With hĭs hand | ŏn my̆ mouth
  He̬ shăll drag | me̬ forth,
Shriĕking | tŏ the̬ south
  And clutch|ĭng at the̬ north.   ←——*Hypersyllabic foot*

The name of any foot holding, as this one does, too many
syllables, is *hypersyllabic*. As with all such devices, it is not an
irregular foot that occurs by chance, but an irregular foot em-
ployed for the sake of some effect in the poem. Here, clearly,

at the last outburst between life and nothing, the speaker is appropriately filling and even brimming the final moment with syllables.

When such an overabundance of syllables occurs at the very beginning of the line — that is, at the beginning of the first foot — it is called *anacrusis*. One of the songs from Shakespeare's *Twelfth Night*, a dozen lines, is written in a prevailing trochaic meter, and each line — except for the first two — begins with the heavy opening stress of the trochaic foot.

Anacrusis ⟶ Ŏ mistréss | miné, whére | aré yŏu | roamĭng?
Anacrusis ⟶ Ŏ, stay ănd | hear, yŏur | trué lŏve's | comĭng,
That căn | sing both | high ănd | low.
Trip nŏ furthĕr, prettў sweetĭng;
Journĕys end ĭn lovĕrs meetĭng,
Evĕry wisĕ măn's son dŏth know.

What ĭs love? 'Tĭs not hereaftĕr.
Presĕnt mirth hăth presĕnt laughtĕr;
What's tŏ come ĭs still ŭnsure.
In dĕlay thĕre lies nŏ plentў;
Then come kiss mĕ, sweet-ănd-twentў,
Youth's ă stuff wĭll not ĕndure.

The majority of the lines are regular trochaic. Lines 3, 6, 9, and 12 end with what you now know is a catalectic final foot. The two instances of anacrusis, as indicated, occur in lines 1 and 2.

Each kind of line and foot offers something to the tone of the poem and thus to its felt effect. The pure lines offer steadiness; the four impure lines, with catalexis, offer a way of partitioning what is being said, encouraging the reader's feeling that the "argument" has the strength of logic, and logic's progression; and the two instances of anacrusis, those unnecessary and imploring O's, an excess, begin the song with the splash of longing and urgency, without which the song would be only the argument.

I have said previously that there is no foot without a heavy stress. That is true, and not true. There is something called the *pyrrhic* foot, which is composed of two light stresses. The pyrrhic foot appears in Greek and Roman poetry; in English verse it occurs only when immediately followed by a spondee, and the two feet together are called a *double ionic*. Here is a rare example, again from "Moriturus":

> Here is | the wish
> Of one | that died
> Like a | beached fish   ←——— *Double ionic*
> On the ebb | of the tide. . . .

One more device of progression and hesitation is worth our attention here: the employment of a pause, within the line, at a logical break. Some mark of punctuation will be given, to verify and intensify the pause, before the poem moves on. This pause is called a *caesura*, and in scansion it is *not* counted, though it is certainly meant to be felt. Milton used it frequently:

> But now at last the sacred influence
> Of light appears, ‖ and from the walls of Heav'n
> Shoots farr into the bosom of dim Night
> A glimmering dawn; ‖ here Nature first begins
> Her fardest verge, ‖ and *Chaos* to retire. . . .

(Paradise Lost, Book II)

And here is Shelley:

> I met a traveller from an antique land
> Who said: Two vast and trunkless legs of stone
> Stand in the desert . . . ‖ Near them, on the sand. . . .

("Ozymandias")

A CAUTION

In the employment of each of these embellishments and opportunities, the inflection of the lines always follows the pattern of natural speech — it never, never betrays the correct pronunciation of any word.* This we can count on. But, also, we must remember that the pitch and tone of the human voice is multidimensional, while in the mechanics of scansion we have only three indicators: the heavy stress, the light stress, and the spondee. The heavy stresses in any line are not apt to be equal, therefore, though they will be heavier than any of the light stresses. One must remember, always, the two forces that rule here: sense, and pattern.

SUMMATION

You now know most of the rules.

---

*Perhaps it is worthwhile mentioning one more time the fact that many words may be pronounced correctly in more than one way. And also to recall that language is lively and not static; proper pronunciation of words may change over the years.

4

Design: Line Length

Poets are free to select their own designs (within the rules, I mean) and, among all the options, to determine the brevity or the extravagance of their lines. But they rarely do — they rarely go beyond the usual. In truth, much has been tried, and much has failed. What works, works for profound and understandable reasons. And so the workable formulae have become the formal structures which are used and used again.

The reason why these usual line lengths work is that they inform the reader of a tone or mood, and thus help to persuade the reader toward the idea in the poem. Line length is an active, never a neutral, part of the process of writing.

We *say* the poem, whether we speak it aloud or in the back room of the mind; therefore, we *read* the poem and, hearing it, we *breathe* it. And we breathe it in linear fashion, since that is the way it is presented to us. So our breathing (and our hearing) fit themselves to the length of the line and its "message." The message of an eight-foot line is very different from the message of the two-foot line, or the dancing three-foot line. Thus we can speak of the "message" of the line length.

More poems in English literature are constructed with the five-foot line than with any other length of line. The work of Spenser, Marlowe, Shakespeare, Milton, and Wordsworth, to name a few, rests upon the foundation called pentameter. The secret of its constant employment is simply that it is the line which is the closest to the breathing capacity of our lungs — we have just enough breath on one uninterrupted reach to say it through — at the end we are neither exhausted nor do we have any real amount of breath left. It fits us. Thus the message it delivers is a message of capability, aptitude, and easy fulfillment, not edginess, not indolence, but the ease of something that fits — the ease of the song that fits, that one sings calmly. Within it passion, great passion, is held in the wildfire of form.

Farewell! thou art too dear for my possessing. . . .

Shakespeare begins Sonnet 87 using such a five-foot line, which lingers an instant within itself, with its feminine tag. Yet, what is he saying? That to hold on to his love is impossible, that he is going to lose his love. And also (we hear this in the pentameter line) he is saying an additional thing — that he is going to face this loss and this anguish with dignity; he is not going to rail or weep; he is saying that it is a grief too deep for weeping, too dear for railing; he is going to *speak* about it — about love and loss — with courage and with grace. He has chosen for this task the pentameter line. And we can expect therefore that we are not going to be bruised, and trod upon, but rather elevated, instructed; we are going to be witness to humanity at its best, to capability in spite of great grief.

This is also the message of doomed Keats's heavily laden sonnet:

THE RULES

Bright star, would I were stedfast as thou art. . . .

Or these lines, by Sir Philip Sidney:

> Come, Sleep; O Sleep! the certain knot of peace,
> The baiting place of wit, the balm of woe,
> The poor man's wealth, the prisoner's release,
> Th' indifferent judge between the high and low. . . .
>
> (*Astrophel and Stella,* Sonnet 39)

Lines shorter than pentameter leave the reader feeling slightly hurried and, thus, agitated. You might think that the opposite, a sense of relaxation, would be felt, since there is more breath left with the shorter line. But it is not so. We speak briefly when a sense of urgency is upon us, when we are pitched to some emotion sharper than contemplation. We reach, in ceremony or in thought, for the complete; we reach, in emotion, for the succinct.

And here we see how forceful is the pattern's work upon us, for we quickly, within a line or two, believe the pattern that is given; we put on its "atmosphere" and adjust our mood according to the length of the line. It is amazing. And it is reliable.

Even as pentameter is suitable to the construct of meditation, an ordering of emotion, so tetrameter is well suited to "story" poems — poems in which there is movement, confrontation, action. Frost's "Stopping by Woods on a Snowy Evening" is tetrameter:

> Whose woods these are I think I know.
> His house is in the village though;

He will not see me stopping here
To watch his woods fill up with snow.

A sense of restlessness, unsettledness, moves us forward; something is not quite right, and it wants to be resolved. Which is, indeed, what the poem is about. The poem is empowered, in part, by the tetrameter lines.

The traditional ballad stanza is made up of two tetrameter lines (lines 1 and 3) and two trimeter lines (lines 2 and 4), increasing the forward motion even more:

> There lived a wife at Usher's well,
>   And a wealthy wife was she;
> She had three stout and stalwart sons,
>   And sent them o'er the sea.

(Anonymous)

Emily Dickinson's use of this form, in her anxious and iron-willed lyrics, is a part of the narrative believability of her poems. It is the ballad form become the Protestant hymn stanza become the Dickinson luminosity, which seems always to have been uttered just above last gasp:

> I died for Beauty — but was scarce
> Adjusted in the Tomb
> When One who died for Truth, was lain
> In an adjoining Room —

Millay's poem "Moriturus," in dimeter, rings with the swinging back and forth between the two strikings, like the heart with its double beat:

>   If I could have
>   Two things in one:
>   The peace of the grave,
>   And the light of the sun. . . .

But, finally, the process of oiling the wheels, of increasing speed, agitation and excitation, fails. A poem in monometer is almost not a poem. Without any sort of repeated pattern in the line, it fails of energy:

>   Thus I
>   Pass by
>   And die:
>   As One,
>   Unknown
>   And gone. . . .

>   (Robert Herrick, "Upon His Departure")

Adding to the line length, increasing it from pentameter to hexameter, heptameter, octameter even, creates very different effects, as one might suppose. Gone, again, is that sense of calm intelligence, of a construct exactly right for eloquent and unhurried meditation.

Instead the longer line gives a feeling of abundance — sometimes with a sense of energy and brimming over, at other times with a feeling of extraordinary authority and power.

A six-foot line made up only of iambic feet is called an alexandrine. That such a line is different indeed from the pentameter is illustrated by Pope, in his "discussion" of writing style:

If crystal streams 'with pleasing murmurs creep,'
The reader's threatened (not in vain) with 'sleep.'
Then, at the last and only couplet fraught
With some unmeaning thing they call a thought,
A needless Alexandrine ends the song,
That, like a wounded snake, drags its slow length along.

("An Essay on Criticism")

Working with lines in lengths beyond the pentameter, except for the occasional hexameter as above, is perilous work; so quickly, along this longer line, is the sense of poetic language — language compressed — lost. Edgar Allan Poe uses an octameter line in the pattern of "The Raven," but gives at least some of the eight-foot lines an internal rhyme, so that in fact the perceived length is actually that of two four-foot lines:

Once upon a midnight dreary, while I pondered, weak
   and weary,
Over many a quaint and curious volume of forgotten
   lore —
While I nodded, nearly napping, suddenly there came
   a tapping,
As of someone gently rapping, rapping at my chamber
   door —
"'Tis some visitor," I muttered, "tapping at my
   chamber door —
     Only this and nothing more."

In "The Raven" there is little feeling of natural speech, which is not at all Poe's aim at any time. The long lines, even with their internal rhymes, speak of poetry composed, of its sparkling artificiality, of what the poet can *make* rather than what he can *say*. This kind of excitation of the reader's spirit by composition was not the aim of the sonnet writers, who walked the firm pentameter line. That line, five feet, is less a thrust or a fling than it is a natural gesture, a sweet force, vigorous but not too vigorous. It does not say: here is something composed; but, rather: here is something thought, then followed, until it came to its almost inevitable fruition.

5

Release of Energy
Along the Line

THE ENERGY RELEASED across any line of poetry may remain steady, it may accelerate, or it may slacken. This release changes with any change in line length, and with any change from the prevailing pattern to a variant meter. Such a "manipulation" of energy affects tone, and is part of the significant usefulness of variation.

In Byron's "So, We'll Go No More A-Roving," such changes occur in a majority of the lines, and not randomly but with precise intent.

So, We'll Go No More A-Roving

I

Sŏ, we'll gó | nŏ moré | ă-rovĭng
Sŏ laté | ĭntó | thĕ night,́
Thoŭgh thĕ heart́ | bĕ stilĺ | ăs lovĭng,
Ánd thĕ moón | bĕ stilĺ | ăs bright.́

II

Fŏr thĕ swórd | oŭtweárs | ĭts sheáth,
Ănd thĕ soúl | weárs oút | thĕ breást,
Ănd thĕ heárt | mŭst paúse | tŏ breáthe,
Ănd lóve | ĭtsélf | hăve rést.

Thŏŭgh thĕ níght | wăs madé | fŏr lóvĭng,
Ănd thĕ dáy | retúrns | tŏo soón,
Yĕt we'll gó | nŏ móre | ă-róvĭng
Bў thĕ líght | ŏf thĕ moón.

In ten of twelve instances in this trimeter poem, the line begins with an anapestic first foot, then settles into the less energetic iambic to finish the line. Only lines 2 and 8 are altogether iambic; the first of these speaks of the late night, the second of the necessity of rest.

Thus each line with its anapestic first foot starts with a little rush of energy, of esprit; at the change, one doesn't react to the incoming calm iambic so much as one feels the failure of the anapestic meter to continue — its discontinuance "says," rhythmically, that the speaker's energy (like his youth) has run out — and one feels this poignantly over and over each time the poet enters the line with a rising energy that he cannot sustain. Especially poignant is the final line in which (at last) the anapestic *is* repeated; but, it would seem, at the cost of length, for the third foot is absent, as though the effort of two anapests has left the speaker without enough reserve even for the final iamb.

This being so, we read the last line at a slower pace, to drag its brevity to the expected length, and thus the two anapests, clambering to rise, are inevitably dragged down. Altogether the poem expresses, in its meter, the same clash of wish and fact as is expressed in the poet's actual bittersweet words.

Poe's strange, melancholy poem "Annabel Lee" is another example of the extreme effects that the meter can, in daring hands, produce. All through this thirty-six-line poem the line begins with anapests and, as in the Byron poem, settles at last, or "sinks" here and there, to the iambic. In this case, however, the iambic seems the *reasonable* meter — there is so much effort by the anapests, and dactyls too, to lift energy — to cause just that excitation of the mind Poe considered essential in a poem — until the iambic feet begin to seem like small, calm islands in a turbulent ocean.

> It was man|y and man|y a year | ago,
> In a king|dom by | the sea,
> That a mai|den there lived | whom you | may know
> By the name | of Ann|abel Lee; —
> And this mai|den she lived | with no | other thought
> Than to love | and be loved | by me.

And, indeed, the turbulence grows more intense — no line in the first five stanzas reaches its completion without dipping back to the iambic. In the fifth stanza, three of the six lines suddenly break free and do *not* revert to the iambic, but continue across the line their rousing anapests, and in the last stanza every one of the six lines is pure anapestic — twenty-eight uninterrupted anapestic feet, with their lively surging power. Twice they reach the name of Annabel Lee itself and, as has almost but not quite happened in previous lines, the lines now ingest the name in perfect anapestic order, without a single change in meter. By the end of that sixth stanza the reader is transported, by the rhythm, by the unnatural, composed, pressuring rhythm, straight out of this reasonable world and into the delirium, the opulence, the mythology, the rich and endless night of a different order.

Such matters — the line, the energies of the line rising or falling — are no small part of the power of the poem. The concretions of composition, narrative and *form*, are so powerful.

6

Design: Rhyme

RHYME — that decisive repetition of sound at the end of lines — gives the kind of pleasure felt with any anticipation and arrival. We learn from the early lines of the poem when to expect the rhyming sound; we feel pleasure as each rhyming unit is brought to its fruition; our pleasure increases throughout the poem each time we anticipate the rhyme, and wait for it, and are not disappointed. It is the closing of the perfectly fitting lid upon the delicate box. It is the sound the tumblers make in the lock as the combination is given, and they click their respect for order as they spin and find their place.

There are several kinds of rhyme. The strongest is the *couplet* — rhyme which occurs in consecutive lines — and it is at its boldest when it occurs in the form of *true* rhyme (or, as it is also called, *perfect* rhyme), in which the words rhyme exactly. Here is Blake again:

> Tyger! Tyger! burning bri<u>ght</u>　　　(*a*)
> In the forests of the ni<u>ght</u>. . . .　　(*a*)

Here each of the rhyming words has the same inner sound, preceded by a different consonant sound. Each is a one-syllable word and is therefore heavily stressed; by this definition it is *masculine* rhyme. Such masculine and true rhymes naturally achieve the deepest possible emphasis and effect.

Words of more than one syllable that end with a lightly stressed syllable create what is called *feminine* rhyme. Here is Byron:

> Oh, talk not to me of a name great in story;   (*a*)
> The days of our youth are the days of our glory;   (*a*)
> (Lord Byron, "All for Love")

Here the rhyme is deliciously present, but lighter in force than the masculine rhyme above.

The longer the line, the milder the effect of the rhyme, as it takes us that much longer to reach the closure. The first example below is tetrameter; the second only a foot longer:

> And since to look at things in bloom   (*a*)
> Fifty springs are little room,   (*a*)
> About the woodlands I will go   (*b*)
> To see the cherry hung with snow.   (*b*)
> (Housman, "Loveliest of Trees")

> There sleeps Titania sometime of the night,   (*a*)
> Lull'd in these flowers with dances and delight; (*a*)

And there the snake throws her enamell'd skin,   (*b*)
Weed wide enough to wrap a fairy in. . . .   (*b*)

(Shakespeare, *A Midsummer Night's Dream*)

The *heroic couplet* is composed of two consecutive lines which rhyme and which express within them a single completed thought; at the end of the two lines, therefore, some punctuation will appear. Traditionally the heroic couplet is written in iambic pentameter. Here is Pope, master of the heroic enclosure:

A vile conceit in pompous words expressed,   (*a*)
Is like a clown in regal purple dressed;   (*a*)

or

True ease in writing comes from art, not chance,   (*a*)
As those move easiest who have learned to dance.   (*a*)

("An Essay on Criticism")

In such writing, the second line of each unit (couplet) is necessarily end-stopped, or *self-enclosed* — in immediate thought or grammar, it has come to a conclusion. The reader may even be inclined to pause for an instant. By contrast, lines in other writing may continue the thought over the first line and into the second, and perhaps beyond the second, creating an altogether less emphatic sense of completion and formality, and even a little rumpling of the feeling of the measure — if nothing has come to a completion at the end of the line, the reader is likely to *hurry* on to the next line. This is called *enjambment*. Here is a fairly mild but noticeable example:

> A thing of beauty is a joy for ever: (*a*)
> Its loveliness increases; it will never   (*a*)
> Pass into nothingness; but still will keep   (*b*)
> A bower quiet for us, and a sleep   (*b*)
> Full of sweet dreams, and health, and quiet breathing. (*c*)
>
>   (Keats, "A Thing of Beauty")

Here, after the initial line, phrases conclude internally rather than at the ends of the lines, and the lines therefore swing rapidly from the right back to the left. There is, in this passage, no extreme breakage of the small phrases of logic or grammar — such breakage seems to be a modern trait. Contemporary non-metrical poems are full of it, and perhaps wisely so. Without meter, this ability to manipulate the speed of the line turn is even more inviting than in the metrical poem, where it operates as a viable counterpoint to the tempo of the ongoing metrical pattern.

    When the lines are of various lengths and do not contain within their twinning any regular measure, rhyme with a light, sweet (yet unbreakable) touch is created:

> This is the ship of pearl, which, poets feign,   (*a*)
>   Sails the unshadowed main, —   (*a*)
>   The venturous bark that flings   (*b*)
> On the sweet summer wind its purpled wings   (*b*)
> In gulfs enchanted, where the Siren sings,   (*b*)

And coral reefs lie bare,   (c)
Where the cold sea-maids rise to sun their streaming hair.... (c)

(Oliver Wendell Holmes, "The Chambered Nautilus")

Two words of corresponding sound create a rhyme, but the rhyme may of course go on in additional lines. In Robert Frost's poem "Bereft" (p. 4), the rhyme pattern is a definite part of the poem's evocation of despair and spiritual stagnation — five times the line ends on the same rhyming sound before the poem manages to move on to a second rhyming sound — and then it recovers itself to no reliable pattern but, once again, gets almost paralyzed upon this second rhyme. And so on, to the end of the poem. In "The Chambered Nautilus," on the other hand, the rhyming pattern, at the end of the unequal measures, is only lightly noticed and lightly felt. No two rhyming patterns could be more different, more obviously intended for different effects. So various are the possible uses of corresponding sound.

All of the rhyming sounds in the examples given so far are exact or true rhymes. This preciseness of sound, crisp and emphatic, is the most commonly used. But there are other kinds, and degrees, of rhyming.

Slant rhyme (or off-rhyme, or imperfect rhyme) also occurs frequently. In slant rhyme, the rhyming words have a similar but not an identical inner vowel sound: "clack" and "black" are true rhymes; "clack" and "bleak" are slant rhymes. The effect of slant rhyme is to create the usual clasping instant, but it is less simple, less emphatic than the closure of true rhyme — as though it were darkened by some disturbance, some complexity. One is apt to hear in true rhyme a cheerfulness and sense of resolution; in slant rhyme one hears a minor key. Emily Dickinson often used slant rhyme. So did Wilfred Owen:

> For his teeth seem for laughing round an <u>apple</u>. (*a*)
> There lurk no claws behind his fingers <u>supple</u>;   (*a*)
>   ("Arms and the Boy")

An even more intense form of slant rhyme appears when "matched" words have similar but not exact inner vowel sounds and the same initial and final consonant sound. Again, the example is from Owen's poem "Arms and the Boy":

> Let the boy try along this bayonet <u>blade</u>   (*a*)
> How cold steel is, and keen with hunger of <u>blood</u>. . . . (*a*)

Feminine rhyme is of course double rhyme; "story"/"glory" used in the Byron couplet (p. 41) is a two-syllable or double rhyme. When double rhyme is used extensively (as in *The Song of Hiawatha* where, page after page, it is the only rhyme, completing the final trochaic foot), it becomes a fairly overwhelming presence, a music that loses its suppleness in the rigidity of its exact duplication for so long a time. It becomes *too* noticed.

There is also *triple* rhyme, as in the following:

> Ah, distinctly I <u>remember</u> it was in the bleak <u>December</u>. . . .
>   (Poe, "The Raven")

At least theoretically, four-syllabled rhyme also exists. But with such lengthy collaboration of syllables we are pretty much out of the deep water of serious poems and into the chuckling shallows of lighthearted verse and word games, where the rhyming is more ornamental than seriously useful.

Multisyllabled rhymes, in poems serious or foolish, may be made up of words of unequal syllabic length, so long as the syllabic stresses work out correctly. Thus one may come upon rhymes like the following:

> And then my heart with pleasure fills,
> And dances with the daffodils . . .
>
> > (Wordsworth, "I Wander'd Lonely . . .")

or

> In May, when sea-winds pierced our solitudes,
> I found the fresh Rhodora in the woods . . .
>
> > (Emerson, "The Rhodora")

or even

> Thou on whose stream, mid the steep sky's commotion,
> Loose clouds like earth's decaying leaves are shed,
> Shook from the tangled boughs of Heaven and Ocean. . . .
>
> > (Shelley, "Ode to the West Wind")

When metrical poems are written down in the units called stanzas, the initial group of lines sets the design to be followed, establishing the metrical pattern, the line length or lengths, and the system of rhyme. The four-line stanza (or *quatrain*) is the most common. It may have one rhyming pair of lines and one unrhyming (*a,b,c,b*), or it may have two rhymes (*a,b,a,b*). There is no one rule about line length; sometimes all lines are the same, sometimes not:

> Ŏ mў Luve's likĕ ă reď, reď rōse, (*a*)
>   That's newlў sprung ĭn Junĕ: (*b*)
> Ŏ mў Luve's likĕ thĕ mélŏdiĕ (*c*)
>   That's sweetlў playeď ĭn tunĕ. (*b*)
>
>   (Robert Burns, "A Red, Red Rose")

or

> Therĕ liveď ă wifĕ ať Usher's welĺ, (*a*)
>   Anď ă wealthў wifĕ wăs shé; (*b*)
> Shĕ haď threĕ stouť anď stalwărt sons, (*c*)
>   Anď senť thĕm o'er thĕ sea. (*b*)
>
>   (Anonymous, "The Wife of Usher's Well")

The employment of two rhyming pairs of lines holds the poem in a strict formality. It is of course more difficult to write, but the enjoyment of rhyming closure is doubled:

> Strew ŏn hĕr rosés, rosĕs, (*a*)
> Anď nevĕr ă spraý ŏf yew. (*b*)
> Ĭn quiĕt shĕ repŏsĕs: (*a*)
> Ah! woulď thăt Í dĭd too! (*b*)
>
>   (Matthew Arnold, "Requiescat")

or

He stood, and heard the steeple   (*a*)
   Sprinkle the quarters on the morning town.   (*b*)
One, two, three, four, to market-place and people (*a*)
   It tossed them down.   (*b*)

                       (Housman, "Eight O'Clock")

Another way to pattern the rhymes of a four-line stanza is with one inner and one outer rhyme; that is, *a,b,b,a.* Tennyson uses this scheme throughout his book-length poem *In Memoriam.*

       Behold, we know not anything;   (*a*)
        I can but trust that good shall fall (*b*)
        At last — far off — at last, to all, (*b*)
       And every winter change to spring. (*a*)

Poems written this way feel a little different from poems that use the previous patterns. Perhaps it is the long reach of the outer rhyme (the ear waits longer) surrounding the shorter reach of the inner rhyme (which is actually a couplet) that gives such stanzas a sense of their own completion, compared with the flow of the *a,b,c,b* and the *a,b,a,b* patterns.

Additional rhyming patterns are used in longer stanza arrangements, in the sonnet, and in other traditional forms, which are discussed in the following chapter.

BLANK VERSE

Blank verse is traditionally iambic pentameter without rhyme. Poets have used it for short poems — Frost's "Mending Wall" is written in blank verse — and for longer poems as well. Milton's *Paradise Lost* and Wordsworth's *Prelude* are also written in blank verse. So are the plays of Marlowe and the plays of Shakespeare. Therefore, and easily, one may say without challenge that blank verse — iambic pentameter and no rhyme, though of course with many of the other language and poetic devices exquisitely employed — is the main highway of English poetic language.

7

Design: Traditional Forms

SOME FORMAL DESIGNS are centuries old. The *sonnet* (a little song) was originally an Italian form; sonnets were written by Petrarch long before the form was used by Shakespeare.

The Petrarchan sonnet, fourteen lines long, is made up of two parts, an eight-line section *(octave)* followed by a six-line section *(sestet)*. These two parts may be, but are not always, separated by a line of space. In usual practice, the octave sets forth a situation, or a question; the sestet "solves" it, or in some cohesive or resonant way comments upon this original premise. The rhyme scheme of the Petrarchan sonnet is exact and difficult. The octave pattern is *a,b,b,a a,b,b,a* — that is, the eight-line octave operates with two rhyming sounds. The sestet's design varies; it may be *c,d,e c,d,e* or it may be *c,d,c d,c,d.*

The sonnet is slightly less rigid in the English or Shakespearean version, which loosens these patterns somewhat. It is still a poem of fourteen lines and it is still written traditionally in iambic pentameter. But the design of the rhyme is less fearsome; the English or Shakespearean sonnet is composed of three quatrains and a final couplet. Thus, with an occasional variation in the third quatrain, the pattern is *a,b,a,b c,d,c,d e,f,e,f g,g.*

Of the sonnet we expect both gravity and scintillation. Our inheritance of Shakespeare's sonnets, as well as work by Sidney, Donne, Milton, Wordsworth, Keats, and Shelley, places the sonnet in this special category. So much has been said — memorably — within its mere fourteen lines! The form is comfortably recognizable. The composure of the pentameter; the progression of thought through the quatrains; the "turn" between octave and sestet, as though back into a mirror; the extravagance and yet applicability of its imagery — these are all unforgettable. After a little reading of sonnets, we count the lines no more, but feel what is being said developing toward a wholeness, and know, reliably, when it has come.

Contemporary poets have treated the sonnet with both deference and an iconoclastic spirit of experimentation. Millay wrote a few sonnets in tetrameter and also a sequence using an alexandrine as the final line. Some contemporary sonnets have fewer than fourteen lines, some have more. Such poems break from the rules of design but remain (or intend to remain) true to the nature and spirit of the sonnet — which, in our age, includes its illustrious history. Gerard Manley Hopkins's shining poem "God's Grandeur," although written in a particularly individual style, is a sonnet. So, fittingly, in the first act of the play, are the first fourteen lines of conversation between Romeo and Juliet.

The *ballad* form is suggestive rather than rigid. More often than not, the ballad will be written in four-line stanzas, and the line lengths will alternate between tetrameter (lines 1 and 3) and trimeter (lines 2 and 4). But this is not necessarily so. Sometimes the stanza will have one pair of rhymes, sometimes two. Occasionally an additional line, called a *refrain,* is attached to the end of each stanza. This line is also, sometimes, called the *burden.*

Since the ballad was orally remembered and transmitted from one listener to another, and often in association with music (and, thus, an individual performer), there are often many slightly different versions of the same ballad. Ballads make use of dialect, and of obsolete words, the correct pronunciation of which — besides the meaning — is no common matter. This is a part of the difficulty of enjoying ballads — and also, of course, a part of their richness.

Poets no longer write ballads; they cannot, since the world in which ballads were a rich, weird, and real part of everyday life no longer exists. Some poets do, however, still write literary ballads.

No one knows who wrote the traditional ballads. They were, no doubt, a multitude — of singers, and storytellers.

You will recall that two rhyming lines are called couplets. In a continuation of this logic, three rhyming lines are called *tercets:*

> The wrinkled sea beneath him crawls;
> He watches from his mountain walls,
> And like a thunderbolt he falls.

> (Tennyson, "The Eagle")

The same word, *tercet,* is used for a three-line stanza that does not rhyme, or rhymes only partially.

Terza rima utilizes such a three-line stanza. It is traditionally a poem in iambic pentameter, with a rhyming pattern *a,b,a b,c,b c,d,c,* etc., with no pause or sense of completion, necessarily, in either statement or grammar, between tercets. There is, rather, a strong sense of movement forward. In Shelley's "Ode to the West

THE RULES

Wind," four tercets are followed by a single couplet, this arrangement of lines making up a single self-contained portion of his spirited and breathy ode.

> . . .
>
> Drive my dead thoughts over the universe   (*a*)
> Like withered leaves to quicken a new birth!   (*b*)
> And, by the incantation of this verse,   (*a*)
>
> Scatter, as from an unextinguished hearth   (*b*)
> Ashes and sparks, my words among mankind! (*c*)
> Be through my lips to unawakened earth   (*b*)
>
> The trumpet of a prophecy! O, Wind,   (*c*)
> If Winter comes, can Spring be far behind?   (*c*)

The *villanelle*, originally and still a French form, is a poem of nineteen lines, set out in five tercets and a final quatrain. The poem works on only two rhymes; the first line and the third line of the initial stanza are repeated, exactly or almost exactly, throughout the rest of the stanzas, as follows: *a,b,a a,b,a a,b,a a,b,a a,b,a a,b,a,a.* A better bet is to look at Elizabeth Bishop's villanelle "One Art," in the anthology section of this book.

As you might expect, given their rigid form, villanelles are not common. They are usually, but not always, in iambic pentameter.

The *Spenserian stanza* is a nine-line unit; the first eight lines are iambic pentameter, and the final line is an alexandrine — a six-foot line in perfect iambic. The rhyming pattern is *a,b,a,b,b,c,b,c,c.* Edmund Spenser stitched together this stanza

for *The Faerie Queene.* The effect of the first eight lines is, natu-
rally, that of a reliable regularity; the longer reach of the final
line, even though longer by only one foot, is useful and richly
surprising. Keats elected to use this stanza for his long and lush
poem "The Eve of St. Agnes."* Pentameter moves the story
forward — the lovers meet, they feast, the hour grows late; a
sense of danger builds. Yet with each stanza that single longer
line holds them back, there is an anchor in it, a drag, a lag, which
deepens the story and the felt suspense — will the two lovers
escape or not?

XXXIX

'Hark! 'tis an elfin-storm from faery land,
Of haggard seeming, but a boon indeed:
Arise — arise! the morning is at hand; —
The bloated wassillers will never heed: —
Let us away, my love, with happy speed;
There are no ears to hear, or eyes to see, —
Drown'd all in Rhenish and the sleepy mead:
Awake! arise! my love, and fearless be,
For o'er the southern moors I have a home for thee.'

XL

She hurried at his words, beset with fears,
For there were sleeping dragons all around,
At glaring watch, perhaps, with ready spears —

---

*The poems included in the anthology section are primarily for illustration,
and length was necessarily a consideration. Had it not been, "The Eve of St.
Agnes" would have been one of the first poems chosen.

Down the wide stairs a darkling way they found. —
In all the house was heard no human sound.
A chain-droop'd lamp was flickering by each door;
The arras, rich with horseman, hawk, and hound,
Flutter'd in the besieging wind's uproar;
And the long carpets rose along the gusty floor.

There are other exacting traditional forms. Many metrical poems, of course, are not so detailed, but evolve through the continuing four-line stanza, or by simple continuance, one line following another, the meter alone the principal support of a requisite formality. Or, a poet may regale out of the language a nameless but appropriate design for a particular poem. John Donne's "Song" and George Herbert's "The Flower" stand formal and metered, but there is no name for their designs. Coleridge, in "Kubla Khan," suddenly and dramatically changes line length; such refusal of regulation emphasizes the wildness of the poem's landscape. The stanza that Shelley uses in "To a Skylark" also has no name — a twice-rhymed quatrain of trimeter lines, then an alexandrine ascending:

All the earth and air
    With thy voice is loud,
As, when night is bare,
    From one lonely cloud
The moon rains out her beams, and Heaven is overflowed.

What thou art we know not;
    What is most like thee?
From rainbow clouds there flow not

Drops so bright to see,
As from thy presence showers a rain of melody.

Like a Poet hidden
In the light of thought,
Singing hymns unbidden,
Till the world is wrought
To sympathy with hopes and fears it heeded not. . . .

8

Words on a String

ALONG WITH metrical correctness and fluidity, patterned poems retain the usual need for other language devices, which make poems a sweet and memorable honey on the tongue and in memory. Alliteration and assonance are as potent here as anywhere, and their richness, along the little mountain ranges of the heavy and light stresses, is as desirable here as in any other type of poem.

Alliteration is the repetition of initial sounds of words, as in:

> A sweet disorder in the dress
> Kindles in clothes a wantonness.
>
> (Herrick, "Delight in Disorder")

or

> His head was light with pride, his horse's shoes
>
> Were heavy, and he headed for the barn.
>
> (Richard Wilbur, "Parable")

or

> Because the Holy Ghost over the bent
> World broods with warm breast and with ah! bright wings.
>
> (Hopkins, "God's Grandeur")

Such writing pleases the tongue. It aids memory. It is helpful to the presentation of what is being said: we linger over what we like; we skim briskly what we don't find interesting or attractive or pleasurable.

Assonance involves vowel sounds and the interiors of words. The reading (listening) mind is captivated by repetition, as the same "note," housed inauspiciously inside the words, is struck again and again, as in the following:

> Build thee more stately mansions, O my soul . . .
>
> (Holmes, "The Chambered Nautilus")

or

> He clasps the crag with crooked hands. . . .
>
> (Tennyson, "The Eagle")

The effect of vowels altogether, not repeating but changing in a certain order, opening gradually or closing gradually so that their effect is of darkening or lightening, has no name, but it can create a powerfully felt moment in a poem, as in the following two examples, the first of which closes and darkens in tone, while the second lightens and opens:

Once the ivory box is broken,
Beats the golden bird no more.

(Millay, "Memorial to D.C.")

. . . Round the decay
of that colossal wreck, boundless and bare
The lone and level sands stretch far away.

(Shelley, "Ozymandias")

Onomatopoeia is the use of words that mean exactly what they say — or, rather, what they "sound": birds actually do "chirp," bees actually do "buzz." Many words and phrases, if not truly onomatopoetic in this way, are certainly first or second cousins to it. Wordsworth describes his daffodils

Fluttering and dancing in the breeze. . . .

("I Wander'd Lonely . . .")

Coleridge presents us with the river Alph

Five miles meandering with a mazy motion . . .

("Kubla Khan")

while Frost, in "Stopping by Woods on a Snowy Evening," talks about

. . . the sweep
of easy wind and downy flake . . .

all passages with a haunting sensitivity to sound.

9

Mutes and Other Sounds

SOUND ITSELF (I have said this before) is surely a signifier of mood, and thus of message; each of the twenty-six letters of the alphabet represents a sound with a particular tonal quality. The letters themselves can be divided into a number of groups — vowels and consonants, which are further divided into semivowels, aspirates, liquids, and mutes.

The letters representing mute sounds are *b*; *c*, *k* (hard), and *q*; *d*; *g* (hard); *p* and *t*. Each is a quick whack of a sound, emphatic and vibrationless; each, importantly, is a sound that refuses to elide with any other. "The dogs jump into the car" leaves no felt space between "dogs" and "jump" because there is none. But "The dog jumps into the car" sets up, between the word "dog" and the word "jump," an unfillable instant of nothingness — speech ends on the hard *g* sound and begins again with the *j*, but our actual, physical vocal apparatus cannot make any bridge of sound across the very narrow but *felt* vacuum. It is so with the hard sound of *g* and all the other mute sounds, and it is so with none of the other sounds, or letters.

Such created "silences" within a poem are noticeable, truncating as they do, for an instant, the otherwise unbroken string of sound. Within a line, use of a mute sound is like a tiny swoon, a mini-caesura:

> He watches from his mountain walls,
> And like a thunderbolt he falls.
>   ^
>   (Tennyson, "The Eagle")

At the end of a line, a mute sound naturally deepens the physical pause before the eye sweeps back to the left; it is a snap and a click; it is an enforcer of the self-containment, and so the certainty, of what has been said:

> 'Men work together,' I told him from the heart,
> 'Whether they work together or apart.'   ^
>   ^
>   (Frost, "The Tuft of Flowers")

Other categories of sound create other effects. The liquids *l* and *r* are just that, watery sounds; they suggest softness, fluency, motion. If you want to create a scene of softness and ease, the liquids will be appropriate:

> Pillow'd upon my fair love's ripening breast,
> To feel for ever its soft fall and swell. . . .
>   (Keats, "Bright star, would stay steadfast . . .")

And so it is with each category of sound, with each word. The very letters of the words rasp, or whistle, or sigh. Or shout. Or whisper. Sound is either a help or a hindrance to the poem, for no sound is neutral.

10

The Use of Meter in
Non-Metric Verse

SUSTAINED METRICAL DESIGN does not exist in free-verse poems, of course, but often some meter is employed briefly for effect. Especially one finds meter "happening" at the conclusion of the poems. Such practice is simply evidence of the almost natural usefulness of meter with its repeated rhythms and their reliable effects — the absolute certainty that is created by design. Meter has received no recognition as an adjunct to the cadences of the contemporary non-metrical poem. Yet here it is, for example, at the end of Dylan Thomas's "Fern Hill":

> Nothing I cared, in the lamb white days, that time would
>   take me
> Up to the swallow thronged loft by the shadow of my hand,
>   In the moon that is always rising,
>   Nor that riding to sleep
>   I should hear him fly with the high fields

And wake to the farm forever fled from the childless land.
Oh as I was young and easy in the mercy of his means,
        Time held me green and dying
    Though I sang in my chains like the sea.

Thomas uses the anapest with frequency throughout the poem, and indeed he must, for it is a common pattern appearing, for example, whenever there is a one-syllable preposition followed by an article followed by a one-syllable noun — "in the moon," "to the farm," and "in my chains" are all anapests. But when repeated, the anapest creates something more — a design, an *intent*. Here, at the end of Thomas's rich, lyric lamentation, the three anapests slow down the final line of the poem; they formalize it; they bow to artistry rather than to the patternless running, playing, rising, and falling that are part of the natural physical actions celebrated in the body of the poem.

There are many instances in which the free-verse poem is, for a moment, so formalized. In Henry Reed's non-metrical poem "Naming of Parts," the line concluding the first stanza is

        And today we have naming of parts

and the almost identical line

        For today we have naming of parts

is the last line of the last stanza — a metrical echo — a pressure of meter toward formalization and conclusion.

The two following lines, by Millay,

Once the ivory box is broken,
Beats the golden bird no more . . .

(from "Memorial to D.C.")

are tetrameter; the first line is pure trochaic, the second is trochaic also, with a catalectic final foot. But the lines come at the conclusion of a non-metrical poem.

And so on.

11

The *Oh*s and the *Ah*s

Oh and *Ah* (or *O* and *Ah*), those invitational exhalers of emotion
— those signifiers of ascending emotion and blasted restraint —
appear in poems of all ages and kinds. This, however, is true: in
free verse the poet says *oh* or says *ah* whenever he or she chooses
to do so, while in metrical lines there is, perhaps, a temptation to
say *oh* or *ah* — or not to say it — because it suits an ongoing
pattern. Occasionally the use of such syllables is attached to the
pattern by anacrusis, as in the song "O mistress mine . . ."
(p. 26). More usually, the exclamation is simply one of the toes of
the foot, needed for fit whether or not it is an asset to the tone.

The use of *oh* or *ah* is most believable when it could have
been avoided by the choice of another word, but was chosen
itself instead, as in:

> Why thou were there, O rival of the rose!
>
> (Emerson, "The Rhodora")

Here the presence of the expletive is utterly pleasing; clearly
Emerson could have used any of a hundred one-syllable adjec-
tives, but did not.

There are no rules about such determinations, only the cautions of good sense and good taste. When the use of the exhortation might be judged premature or unsuitable, when it seems to sit at an unripe moment in order to press forth the reader's emotion, a garish sentimentality instantly flows into the poem. But when it is earned, when it is pinned to the line with a calm and grave certainty, then it is choice, and fine:

> Build thee more stately mansions, O my soul
>> (Holmes, "The Chambered Nautilus")

or

> O, for a draught of vintage! that hath been
>> Cool'd a long age in the deep-delved earth . . .
> . . .
> O for a beaker full of the warm South. . . .
>> (Keats, "Ode to a Nightingale")

Use *oh,* and use *ah,* and use them with care. Use them when the feeling of the moment is deep, or exalted; when the poem has made an arrival, or has come to a pitch of longing — when what you want to express needs it, and never when it merely suits the marching orders of the meter.

12

Image-Making

THERE IS LANGUAGE which is literal, discursive, rhetorical. And there is language which is figurative.

Figurative language uses figures — that is, images, "pictures" of things — to provide clarification and intensity of thought. For grace, for illumination, for comparison, to create a language that is vibrant not only with ideas but also with the things of the world that we know through our sense experiences.

> The winds that will be howling at all hours,
> And are up-gather'd now like sleeping flowers. . . .
> (Wordsworth, "The World Is Too Much With Us")

Poetry, imaginatively, takes place within the world. It does not take place on a sheet of paper.

Some figurative language attempts no more (but this is important!) than adding to the objects in the poem the elements of freshness and exactitude. They help us to see:

> And the daughter of Nokomis
> Grew up <u>like the prairie lilies</u> . . .
>
> <div align="right">(Longfellow, <i>The Song of Hiawatha</i>)</div>

or

> We keep the wall between us as we go.
> To each the boulders that have fallen to each.
> <u>And some are loaves and some so nearly balls</u>
> We have to use a spell to make them balance. . . .
>
> (Frost, "Mending Wall")

Metaphor and simile both work through comparison. With simile (the Longfellow lines), one thing is "like" another (or, in the active construction, one thing takes action "as" another thing takes action). With metaphor (the Frost example), the boulders are directly described as loaves and balls, without any expressed comparative word.

Both metaphor and simile may be sweetly simple, or fairly complex, or deeply and elaborately complex.

Here is the opening line from Byron's "The Destruction of Sennacherib":

> The Assyrian came down <u>like the wolf on the fold</u> . . .

and here not only does a visual concurrence happen, but all the other attributes of the wolf devolve upon the warrior: the thoughtlessness, mercilessness, strength and power, the hunter's gladness perhaps — whatever "wolf" means to a reader, beginning with the visual but not confined to it, works in this figure to intensify our sense of the scene.

Milton closes the second book of *Paradise Lost* with the following rich passage, describing Satan's flight from Heaven after the great battle and conference, and then his first glimpse of the earth: "with ease," he writes, Satan

> Wafts on the calmer wave by dubious light
> And like a weather-beaten Vessel holds
> Gladly the Port, though Shrouds and Tackle torn;
> Or in the emptier waste, resembling Air,
> Weighs his spread wings, at leasure to behold
> Farr off th' Empyreal Heav'n, extended wide
> In circuit, undetermined square or round,
> With Opal Towrs and Battlements adorn'd
> Of living Saphire, once his native Seat;
> And fast by hanging in a golden Chain
> This pendant world, in bigness as a Starr
> Of smallest Magnitude close by the Moon.
> Thither full fraught with mischievous revenge,
> Accurst, and in a cursed hour he hies.

What becomes apparent in this passage is that the force of figurative language can be associative and cumulative, as well as astonishing with each individual figure — that we carry an intended swelling residue with us down the page. Striking enough to visualize Satan as a weather-beaten vessel — and perhaps there is a second effect emanating from that word — was Satan not originally the Lord's "vessel"? And how the word "shrouds" flows in two directions, to the image of the sails and to the image of death. The vast space outside Heaven, and the undiscernible shape of Heaven itself, are immensities that accompany us to the final lines, which compose another figure: the earth as Satan first sees it. In all that immensity, it is so tenderly small. Like an ornament, or perhaps a watch (full of time), it hangs in its golden chain, precious (as gold is precious), and "pendant" (dependent? not free and spinning but attached to the hand of the Lord?).

And how chilling, then, that "mischievous revenge" in the mind of Satan as he descends on his "weather-beaten" wings. And, finally, how perfect that Milton gives no figure to help us see the earth itself. This, too, is the work of the poet — to lead the reader forward through the scintillations of figurative language, and then, when it is wise to halt — to halt. Milton could have given us a last glorious figure, no doubt. Instead, each reader is faced at that moment with *seeing*, in a privacy, a Milton-induced intimacy, our sweetest just-created world.

It is possible of course to write a poem without figurative language. And yet . . . What is poetry but, through whatever particular instance seems believably to be occurring, a meditation upon something more general and more profound?

Frost's poem "Stopping by Woods on a Snowy Evening" has no metaphor or simile, no figure; it is no more than precise, and very lovely, description. And yet . . . The poem is surely about more than a simple pause before a winter forest. The whole poem, in fact, is a figure. The traveler is talking both about a particular journey and about all the miles still to be traveled, which are life itself; the traveler's hesitation before the allurement of the deep dark, with its suggestion of rest, is surely the longing of a wearied and uncertain spirit; the "promises" are the responsibilities we either meet or fail. Perhaps Frost made no use of a single figure so that the transcendence of the sixteen lines might more easily be accomplished — that we might savor the entire figure more fully. In any case, there is no mistaking the poem's transcendence from a particular musing and rather melancholy instance to the more profound level of a life decision.

Blake's poem which begins

> And did those feet in ancient time
> Walk upon England's mountains green?
>
> > ("And Did Those Feet")

works in somewhat the same way, not through the delightful presence of figurative language as we usually think of it — similes and metaphors — but through the effect of a sudden, unexplained correspondence. If we miss this, we miss the poem. But we are not likely to miss it. The first two stanzas give us history, and a question — did ever God walk through England, which was once green and pleasant, but which has become dark and satanic? Then, in the wild third stanza,

> Bring me my bow of burning gold!
> Bring me my arrows of desire!
> Bring me my spear: O clouds unfold!
> Bring me my chariot of fire!

we feel the spirit of religion as a roused warrior, arming not with the iron of hate but with "arrows of desire" and a bow of gold. It is a moment Blake wisely gave not to discourse but to passion and outburst — responsibilities so wonderfully fulfilled by figurative language.

Another figurative device is *personification,* in which something inanimate — in order to create an intimacy or a sense, however impossible logically, of an operating will — is made to seem animate. Again, here is the familiar Wordsworth sonnet:

This sea that bares her bosom to the moon . . .

or, from Shakespeare's Sonnet 18,

> Sometimes too hot the eye of heaven shines,
> And often is his gold complexion dimm'd . . .

or, from Wilfred Owen's "Arms and the Boy,"

> Let the boy try along this bayonet-blade
> How cold steel is, and keen with hunger of blood;
> Blue with all malice, like a madman's flash;
> And thinly drawn with famishing for flesh.

A *conceit* is the word used for an extended metaphor — an idea or correspondence that continues, sometimes through an entire poem, rather than occurring swiftly, in a singular instance. Shakespeare's Sonnet 87, which begins

> Farewell! thou art too dear for my possessing . . .

in which the poet speaks about love and the loss of love in exact legalistic terms, is a conceit. Because it is unusual, even fanciful, it is called a *metaphysical* conceit. Conceits that make use of more natural and less surprising comparisons are called *Petrarchan*. Shelley's use of a wild bird as an emblem of imaginative energy, throughout his long poem "To a Skylark," is an example of a *Petrarchan* conceit.

*

Poetry is rich with objects of the natural world used as images, comparisons, or emblematic figures. The force of the physical world upon us — even in our "civilized" state — is beyond measure, and it was even more so in Shakespeare's time, or the age of Keats, or even Frost. Thinking is an exercise that proceeds from experiencing, and the physical world is our arena of experience. We see, hear, smell, taste, touch — and begin the meditation. What is abstract, general, and philosophical is woven with the living fibers of grass, red roses, nightingales, snowy evenings, and dawns.

Our experience with the physical world is assumed — a fact which may, alas, soon be no longer true for some of us. Keats's bright star, or any star, is hardly visible now from many cities, and daybreak is an hour on the watch face rather than the illumination of rosy fingers over the village.

And yet assimilating the experiences and the references of the poetry of the past *requires* that our relationship with the physical world be fresh, forceful, and firsthand. When Donne wrote a poem called "Daybreak," in which he says that the light shining from his lady's eyes is for him the dawn, he is not speaking generally or just prettily — he is making a comparison between two experienced sources of light.

Unless the reader is also experienced with one of these sources of light — the arrival of dawn — the figure (the light of her eyes) for that reader is no more than rhetorical, and no experienceable realization can be received from the figure in the poem. Without knowledge of the natural world, it is poor work trying to read the old poems and "feel" them. No one speaks about this, but it is a real peril. As we remake our world, as we take down the physical surroundings of our past, the art of that past is becoming a "storybook" place and not the real "interface" (to take back an old word) between the lightnings, the blood flows, of passion, language, and thought.

The final device of figurative language to be considered here is *allusion*, which is a reference made in a poem to something more generally known, or exemplary, or of a certain connotation; it is used to swell the importance or gravity of some point in the poem. Keats's reference to "Eremite" in the following lines is an example:

> Bright star, would I were stedfast as thou art —
> Not in lone splendour hung aloft the night
> And watching, with eternal lids apart,
> Like nature's patient, sleepless Eremite,
> The moving waters at their priestlike task. . . .
>
> ("Bright star, would I were stedfast . . .")

In order for the allusion to work, the reader naturally must recognize the reference. Here, as in too many instances, this recognition is unlikely — how many of us know offhand that the Eremite is a religious solitary, a recluse of the third century, a hermit, often a desert dweller? Such lack of recognition is a problem that becomes ever more serious as the fields of classical mythology, history, and religion are less and less generally studied; for these are all fields mined heavily for allusions in the age of metrical poetry.

There is no solution but the pursuit of the particular knowledge that will disclose the meaning of the allusion. Modern poets will never stop using such allusions altogether, for in their tradition and age allusions are solid and powerful, but of course poets are just as apt to use names and other references that are easily familiar to modern readers.

The final poem in the anthology at the end of this book, Emerson's "Uriel," is difficult in its meter, statement, and use of allusions. It is also, or anyway, an unmistakably glorious poem, and it is placed last in the selection not only because it is difficult but because it is so suitable to a place of honor. The small work of conning for an understanding of the allusions will be long finished before the other elements — meter and meaning — release themselves to you in their entirety. It is a mountain of a poem, not to be climbed in a single day. But, begin! You now know the regular and abiding rules of a metrical poem. You now are able to *dance* with it.

Part Two
The Dancers One by One

13

Style

BUT, everywhere you turn, there is the flute of exception that surmounts the rules.

I do not mean that the rules are greatly disobeyed or neglected, but that they are *leaned upon* in such a way that the poem takes on particular and distinct habits of language, of tone and phrasing, and sometimes of scansion displacement, which themselves become almost reliable and characteristic.

That is: the poem has style.

Dancing with Mr. Emerson is not much like dancing with Mr. Blake; certainly it is not like dancing with Mr. Pope or Ms. Dickinson. Each poet, following the abiding rules *more than less,* writes differently from all other poets.

The rules, that is, are somewhat bendable. The poem, that is, has a second source of energy, which is the individual's direction: the individual's sensibility, speech patterns, conscious intent, love of plainness or opulence, and so on.

All significant poets have a distinctive style.

Even Poe, whose poems are so perfect in their scanability, has a style. Or, to put it another way, his meticulous fulfillment of the metrical pattern *is* his style. Poe's poems, flowing without hesitation, answering with utmost neatness each expectation of heavy or light stress, as in "Annabel Lee," excite with a sense of artificiality, polish, and perfection. One feels some small god — no human — is speaking the poems. Which is exactly what Poe wanted — to create that sense of "elevating excitement," as he termed it, which is the result of contemplating Beauty, which exists in perfect Form.

But most poets do not dream of this sort of rigid perfection. Instead, they develop a style with more pliant horizons. They seek, along with the steady rhythm of the metrical pattern, opportunities to create an emphatic counterpoint — that is, to speak within the rhythm with more believable secondary patterns of haste and hesitation — of inflection — than perfect, flowing scanability would allow.

Usually such need leads to simple variation in the pattern, which is why variation is housed with the rules — it is entirely necessary.

Less often, such need leads to irregularity — lame feet, hypersyllabic feet, a little awkwardness or actual stumbling in the line, or some faintly felt but stone-hard hitch in the stream of the language — some nameless but distinct idiosyncrasy. That is: style.

Blake does not always scan cleanly. Coleridge, in "The Rime of the Ancient Mariner," occasionally changes the stanza pattern, adding a line here, using a different rhyme scheme there. It is a great poem all the same. Irregularities are not necessarily errors. They are, simply, exceptions, which may be, in the right hands, exceptional!

But the breakage, or out-breakage, from the pattern is only part of what is meant by style. There are also that tone of voice and habits of speech that are distinctive. Is there any mistaking

Pope's wit, those pithy lines that twirl twice in the air, then close neatly upon their perfect rhyme?

> True ease in writing comes from art, not chance,
> As those move easiest who have learned to dance.
>
> ("An Essay on Criticism")

Is there any mistaking Shelley's voice, a little breathless and sometimes a little pompous too, and likely addressing all four quarters of Heaven, but always sonorous with his passion for those two pantheons, the physical world and the human spirit?

> All the earth and air
>   With thy voice is loud,
> As, when night is bare,
>   From one lonely cloud
> The moon rains out her beams, and Heaven is overflowed.
>
> What thou art we know not;
>   What is most like thee?
> From rainbow clouds there flow not
>   Drops so bright to see,
> As from thy presence showers a rain of melody.
>
> Like a Poet hidden
>   In the light of thought,
> Singing hymns unbidden,
>   Till the world is wrought
> To sympathy with hopes and fears it heeded not. . . .
>
> ("To a Skylark")

Is there any mistaking Frost's characteristic tone, the sudden rhetorical certainties flashing out above the green fields of his vernacular easiness?

> I looked for him behind an isle of trees;
> I listened for his whetstone on the breeze.
>
> But he had gone his way, the grass all mown,
> And I must be, as he had been, — alone,
>
> 'As all must be,' I said within my heart,
> 'Whether they work together or apart.'
>
> ("The Tuft of Flowers")

Which is what style is.

In reading the poets, therefore — and I say this meaningfully rather than "poems" — it is helpful to look for the poet's style, to study it, and to accept it. You may like it or not like it, according to your taste. But it is a part of the poem, and indivisible from it.

The metrical poem needs steadiness; also it needs the occasional surprise; also it needs the individual voice. Moreover, the greatest literature does not strive to be literature. All elements of the poem — meter, sound, sense, and style — are there only to make what is written more reasonable, passionate, and effective.

Orpheus, who did not even seem to think, only to sing, is the ultimate poet.

Your Own Style

will take time. It will reveal itself. You cannot force it.

You can, however, suppress it when it begins to appear, and

this you should guard against. In an effort to be rule-abiding, you may smooth out your own work too fiercely. Just those distinctions that often accrue finally to a style are, at first, often rough and hard to handle. But cherish them. Do you seek small perfections, which are not so hard to come by once you know the rules? Rather be patient, and make room always for those oddities that are your own manner, your own voice.

Your own voice.

Part Three

Scansion, and the Actual Work

14

Scansion: Reading the Metrical Poem

THE POEM IS EVER refreshed on new lips. No poem, therefore, is old. It may have historical niceties, but it is, emphatically, about things that are timeless. All it needs is a hand opening the book and a mind that knows how to begin the flowing and polished motions of reading, as of dance.

Dancing is the art of moving in accord with a pattern. Good dancing is the art of creating embellishment upon this pattern. Which is not a bad analogy with reading metrical verse. One sorts out the pattern, one relies on it, and relaxes from effort to pleasure, one begins to come upon and follow opportunities for counterpoint, flourishes, hesitations, as well as certainties, and repetitions. It is an eloquence that involves total imaginative involvement, both physical and mental.

If words were only words, fit only for mental reception, speech-givers would be careful not to move, since, if this foolish premise was true, movement could only create ruptures or corrosions of our attention. Of course speech-givers *do* move, and their motions are suggestive, invitational, emphatic, wistful, forceful, smooth or jerky, repetitive, and (though utterly mute) eloquent. And the force of their words is strengthened by the movements of their bodies.

Speech-givers also use variety of tone, of volume and, above all, of inflection. The voice drops, it lifts, hurries, lags, it hesitates, it repeats. Again, mere meaning, without the participation of our creature bodies, is inadequate.

The metrical pattern of the poem, which itself creates tone, inflection, emphasis, and velocity, is the vehicle of not only suggestive but also specific felt responses. The little letters on the page only seem to be silent. In their arrangement, and in your ability to read them, they are far more — orators, singers, even, as Shelley said, the "unacknowledged" — and uncommonly musical and wonderful — "legislators of the world."

Reading the metrical poem, you must not fail the pattern. If you fail the pattern, you cannot hear the poem, which is half statement and half the music upon which it is impressed — the one so twined within the other that separation, with vigorous life intact, is impossible. For within that pattern are the dancing motions — pitch, and velocity, and emphasis — that raise the body along with the spirit-lifting words, or weigh down the physical body, its muscles and its breath, along phrases of dolor, or wrath.

Poems will have lapses, if you want to call them that. They might as well be called idiosyncrasies, or signatures of style. For the language of the poem is a living material; it is not rigid. It is something far more complex than a list of instructions, say, which is more easily assembled than a poem and might actually hope to be perfect, in the way of simple things.

If you are reading with a willingness, with an undaunted interest, then the prevailing pattern of sound, once discovered, will not leave you; it will carry you safely across any lame feet, hypersyllabic feet, caesuras, instants where you might wonder if the iamb or the spondee is called for; it will carry you across the little rushes forward from enjambment, little pauses at end punctuation; the fullness of vowels, the closures of mutes, and always the tap and patter of the river running on, with *voice* speaking just above it — a voice that so often seems to be speaking the choice and daring words of your own thoughts, though spoken originally, as poems are, by someone else.

To begin, it is helpful to read through a few lines of a poem, noticing where the heavy accents belong, in a natural way. *Remember:* each foot is composed of a single emphasis (heavy accent) plus details.

Remember also: after you have identified the prevailing meter, you will find some variations. But after the flounce or the leap, the poem will surely return, and quickly, to its pattern.

Read on, read on, as though the meter were a natural event. Let the idea of the poem press upon you with its shapeliness.

Honor the regular and abiding principles of meter, as you now know them. But be ready, also, for the exceptions, and for the exceptional.

Do no violence to correct pronunciation or common-sense inflection. *Remember* that you are reading with care for the sake of elevating the meaning, not for the sake of honoring the meter.

As you read, you work on the meaning while the pattern works on you. When you read the poem thoughtfully, you are a scholar. When you read the poem thoughtfully and feelingly, you are a scholar and a participant.

15

Scansion: Writing the Metrical Poem

DANCING HAPPENS not only with the body but with the mind. What you write down on the page, your succession of words, is the music of the dance.

When the poem begins to lurch and sway, its formality is shaken. When awkwardnesses trip the dancer, pleasure and attention, on the instant, will cease. Under the eye of the struggling reader, your poem has failed.

I am not, of course, talking about matters of style, or habits of expression, or anything else cordial to effectiveness, but, simply, of a pattern that doesn't maintain itself strongly enough — reliably enough — to be a real pattern.

Writing metrical poetry is difficult work, no one ever said otherwise. It does, however, get easier with effort and experience. In the beginning, when you reach a difficult place you will think primarily of pressing forward, grappling for a solution in that forthright but narrow way. After a while you will begin to look for solutions in other ways. You will become more willing to backstep, to rearrange, to rewrite whole patches of the poem in order to move on rhythmically and with eloquence. You will begin to do this — accept rewriting — as the writing itself becomes — not easy, but easier.

Also, the more you work with meter, the more your thought will originally articulate itself — arrange itself — metrically. I had a student once who found it quite possible, while he was writing in pentameter, to speak, also, and altogether, in pentameter. At first it was disarming, then rather too odd for our informal society. His parents nearly went mad.

Still, the point was made. Our nimble minds learn to do, even easily, what at first is extremely difficult.

Begin simply. Begin with iambic meter, pentameter or tetrameter, couplets or quatrains. If you use quatrains, use a single rhyming design (*a*,*b*,*c*,*b*). The double rhyme is twice difficult. It is better to concentrate on feeling out and learning to be loyal to the prevailing pattern, than on the search for rhymes.

Keep line lengths the same, and write only phrases that fit the length of line — hold off using enjambment. There will come a moment when, not consciously but "naturally," you introduce enjambment, for rhyme, or velocity, or surprise. When this happens, you are ready to use it.

Do not overuse variant patterns. This is a major error of beginning writers. The thought is: since the variant patterns exist and you have the words to fit them, why not use them. Truly they must be few if the pattern is to give pleasure. "Stopping by Woods on a Snowy Evening," a magical and flowing poem, is built of sixteen tetrameter lines — sixty-four feet therefore — and each foot is an iambic foot. There are no variant feet in the poem, not one. And certainly much of the effect of this poem rises from its physical construction — the careful and determined and even melancholy steadiness of the iambs against the cold and dark and unanswerable world. Think on it.

Expect to use one hypersyllabic foot in ten years, perhaps. Anacrusis, rarely. Catalexis: often. The double ionic: when the next comet flies over. Caesura: once you start using enjambment, caesura will often become useful — the phrase that does not pause at line's end often wants to come to momentary rest at the heart of the next line.

Do not fill out the lines with adjectives. Horror of horrors! Metrical verse requires adjectives as exact and unexpected as those for any other poem.

As the pattern is discoverable to the reader by faith and intelligence, so it is put down on the page by the writer through faith and intelligence. And, perseverence.

Write so that the flow of the pattern brings out the swing and rap of importance.

Remember the all-important difference between scansion (three levels of intonation possible: heavy, light, and equal) and reading (uncountable levels of tone and emphasis and inflection). Write your poems as a writer must: exactly. Read them as a reader should: flowingly, and intelligently.

Consider each poem a concert, played for multitudes. How many wrong notes will you allow?

Finally, do not humble your thoughts, their length or their complexity. Try to *seem* simple. But do not *be* simple.

16

Yourself Dancing:
The Actual Work

SINCE THIS IS a handbook for writers, I would be remiss if I failed to consider the real work — the actual writing of the poem. Still, I continue, in this chapter, my welcome to readers of poetry. The process of writing is neither dull nor entirely inexplicable, and readers as well as writers should find what is said here interesting enough. Somewhere Emerson criticizes Hawthorne, saying that he "invites his readers too much into his study, opens the process before them. As if the confectioner should say to his customers, 'Now, let us make the cake.'" The caution is hardly applicable here. Certainly a part of the power of the poem is the mystery of its existence altogether, which includes our sense of wonder concerning its strange, almost imperial or numinous quality. A handbook, however, is not so much about the poem in its context of mystery as it is about the sturdy ship in which it sails — we are safe, in these pages, from an overabundance of mysteries revealed. That subject — poetry's deep-cut underground rivers and its clearly celestial purposes — remains for another time. What we honor here is the work.

DISCIPLINE

> Genius at first is little more than a great capacity
> for receiving discipline.
>
> Herr Klesmer in *Daniel Deronda,* George Eliot

When you are starting to write poems, make a schedule of the times you will work, and adhere to it with careful and steadfast exactitude.

In this multifaceted, interruptive, too busy world, the conscious mind often closes down to the merely expedient. This is not true, however, of your invisible and uncharted creative vitality, which is reliably and sleeplessly a chamber of energy, and which, even when you are not aware of it, is full of restiveness and invention.

Whenever you work, *you* (the conscious part of your mind) are summoning *it* (the much greater, richer subconscious part of your mind) to sit down at the desk, that you and it may write the poem together. But your subconscious energy works in accordance with waves and tides very different from conscious intent. It needs, in fact, to know *when* it will be summoned to the actual labor; moreover, it needs to know that you *will* summon it, and reliably.

Conscious energy says, *this* is what I will do, and *now* is when I will do it. Subconscious energy works another way. Let us say you are flying to Bermuda in a week; though you don't consciously think about it all the time, it is always there at the back of your mind, stirring and sparkling. So, too, with subconscious creative energy; it is always there stirring and sparkling — but in this case it is stirring and sparkling toward an active objective: to float upward ideas, words, even phrases. And so this energy arrives, when it is time to write, with much work already done. Though you were busy with tasks — getting through traffic lights, keeping appointments — this part of you has been continually at work. If you prove yourself reliable — if you are always there at the desk as promised — it will grow strong and more fertile; it will arrive with all kinds of offerings. But the dread of preparing, and arriving and being forsaken, is very real. As in a romance, the partnership will flourish with each expectation met, or it will wither with each disappointment.

Naturally, in talking about this preparation, I don't mean that you should not scribble down those occasional fistfuls of words that fly by, sometimes even under the traffic lights. Of course you should catch them, if you can. And in fact, working on a schedule, being loyal to it, increases such instances of easy receipt, as the subconscious, in its happy working state, brims over.

REVISION

> All poetry consists of flashes of the subconscious
> mind and herculean efforts on the part of the
> conscious mind to equal them. This is where
> training comes in. The more expert the poet, the
> better will he fill in the gaps in his inspiration.
> Revising is the act of consciously improving
> what has been unconsciously done.
>
> Amy Lowell, *John Keats*

Revision is absolutely necessary. If something is easily too good to alter, thank the gods, but don't expect it to happen again. Expect, rather, that you will need to improve upon the given, to continue the imperfect formation that your initial work has produced. Which is, after all, what making the poem is all about — to take the passion and, without cooling it, to put it into a form. For such work all the usual assets will help: energy, honesty, patience. But nothing is so helpful as an interest in language that amounts almost to a mania. Indeed, it is essential. For emotion does not elicit feeling. Style elicits feeling.

EXERCISE, AND FUN

Dancers exercise. They dance not only in performance but in preparation for that performance. Also, they have fun. I don't mean slapstick, idle hilarity, but the good humor, the elasticity, that comes from their constant awareness of and interest in motion. They are lighthearted as well as light-footed. Singers exercise, and not dolefully but with concentration and energy. Musicians also. Painters also, without waiting for the immense pressure of an idea, sketch, paint, construct, and enjoy. They play. It was fun, such dancers and artists might say of any whiled-away afternoon, in unembarrassed ease.

With poets, such a scene is difficult to imagine. Poets are *so serious*. As if the world were waiting for them to speak — importantly. Or, perhaps, as if each poem represented a disclosure of some personally meaningful sort, which naturally the speaker would want to display from a stage of sobriety. Who rhymes, who riddles, who makes up sonnets for *fun*?

Alas! Solemnity is the littlest god there is. Purposeless, inert solemnity! Next to him, exercise is the lean arm of lightning. And fun, fountain of mirths, is often the cup of ease, surprise, and good ideas.

> Poetry is not the expression of personality, but
> an escape from personality.
>
> T. S. Eliot

There are two kinds of useful exercises. The first sort is to "play" with technique. Such exercises keep the conscious mind freshly aware of options, and skilled in their employment. Choose a subject, any subject, and write some iambic tetrameter lines, rhyming six times. Make them end-stopped. Write another set, enjambed. Try dactyls, or anapests. In other words, *play* with the patterns. Examine what works, and how it works. Or doesn't. There is no failure in such activity. The intent is to learn — and that, of course, is taking place whenever one puts words to paper.

There is a second benefit, probably more important than the first. Even as the subconscious mind, treated honorably, will work with the conscious mind, so the conscious mind needs to nourish that rich underworld, by "giving" it every detail available concerning form. The more familiar the subconscious is with the patterns, the details of form, the more likely the real work, the first approaching line of words, will arrive — *will select itself* — properly. What we do consciously so deeply affects our first subconscious formulations. And, truly, how much more easily the poem reveals itself when it begins, at the first instance, in a feasible pattern!

> To generalize is to be an idiot. To particularize is
> the great distinction of merit.
>
> William Blake

Another kind of exercising is to start, not by thinking and writing, but by looking. Some pinch of the real world is in every poem. Sometimes whole sweeps and fields of it. Description, especially of the natural world, which is the genesis of metaphor, is at the heart of many a poem. Can you find words to make some living inch of the physical world vigorous, breathy, fibrous? Upon such bright straws the weight of your work leans. As with any enterprise, practice will make you better.

READING

Your best teachers are not the talkers, the demonstrators, the encouragers, and the chiders, but the poets of the past, or in a few cases of the present, whose work stands as example. Read. Read! You can never read enough.

Nor is there any harm in imitating, for a while, the poets you admire, as part of the learning process. It is, for the young poet, an act of admiration. It will do no harm, and the possibility of its doing good is ample. You will learn what can be learned — then you will leave that place, wanting your own territory, though it be mostly, at first, a wilderness.

EDITING

Learn to read your own poems as if you never saw them before. Become your own ferocious and unbribable critic. It is essential.

Such a skill, like all the others, demands much practice. After all, it is *your* poem — how can you read it and not be biased? But you can, and must. You, of all people, must be able to see what is unnecessary and unhelpful in it, though it be some personal touch that is dear to you. And you must equally be able to see what it lacks, that *seems* to be there because it is in your own head, but which simply isn't findable on the page. The poem for you — *your* poem — is freighted with emotion, from the first word. But is the first word, and the next and the next, freighted with emotion sharp enough to make its clear signal to the pulse and mind of someone who does not know you or anything about you? We are, after all, in our poems, writing to strangers.

MODESTY

Always remember that the thing you love is language, poetry, its motion, its good news, the applicability of what it says to a thousand human spirits, or a million; and what you do not care about very much is yourself as the poet. And therefore it is the process that is important, and the body of literature entire, and how it changes us from mere humans into meditative beings. Modesty will give you vigor. It keeps open the gates of prayer, through which the mystery of the poem streams, on its search for form. Just occasionally, take something you have written, that you rather like, that you have felt an even immodest pleasure over, and throw it away.

> The world of imagination is the world of reality.
>
> Gully Jimson in *The Horse's Mouth*, Joyce Cary

Part Four

A Universal Music

17

Then and Now

CAN WISDOM be documented in mere words? Is ecstasy reportable? Is there a way to look upon sorrow quietly, to consider it slowly and in detail, with all the time we require?

Is a poem, which after all is only a literary construct within an imagined framework, a reasonable way to understand the world?

The answer to all of these questions, apparently, is *yes*. If it were not, poetry would have become an art starved in the mists of the past, mysterious and evocative but not intimate, not palpable, not thriving. And likewise the poems themselves — poems written long ago — would have become oddments, footnotes, amusing curiosities, rather than the passionate certainties that they are.

Time is meaningless to a poem; if it is about something that pertains to the human condition, then it is about something of interest to the most modern man, if he is a thoughtful man. Shelley is forever twenty-nine years old, and he is forever summoning us to hear the skylark's shrill song, to feel this aerial passage toward "unbodied joy." Poetry, said Aristotle, said Matthew Arnold — said everybody who ever thought about it — is about truth and seriousness, and it carries its ideas in a superior language in which an inviting and perhaps essential motion is embedded. And such poems, though old, are as rich today as when George Herbert was a boy and sat in the kitchen listening to the conversation between two grown-ups, his mother and his mother's friend John Donne. As rich today as when a man named William Shakespeare wrote the fourteen-line version of the aria over and over, tracing the long and heady rise and fall of love. Nothing in the world has changed.

And as you understand by now, the style of the poems with which this book is concerned is not so formidable as you originally thought. There is method, which you now comprehend, both in the way the form is severe and in the way it relaxes so that a particular voice may develop its own individuality. You understand, now, how and to what effect Frost restrained his natural voice with a shaped and exacting formality. You feel the urgent, joyful physicality and pulse of those praise-poets Herbert and Hopkins. You sit wracked and luminous before the miraculous developments and ravishments of Shakespeare's sonnets. Such are the poems of the past, which are also the poems of the present hour.

As for the poets themselves, let me speak of them in the following final paragraphs.

ENVOI

No poet ever wrote a poem to dishonor life, to compromise high ideals, to scorn religious views, to demean hope or gratitude, to argue against tenderness, to place rancor before love, or to praise littleness of soul. Not one. Not ever.

On the contrary, poets have, in freedom and in prison, in health and in misery, with listeners and without listeners, spent their lives examining and glorifying life, meditation, thoughtfulness, devoutness, and human love. They have done this wildly, serenely, rhetorically, lyrically, without hope of answer or reward. They have done this grudgingly, willingly, patiently, and in the steams of impatience.

They have done it for all and any of the gods of life, and the record of their so doing belongs to each one of us.

Including you.

Part Five

An Anthology of
Metrical Poems

An Anthology of Metrical Poems

WITH ONE EXCEPTION, the poems appear in this anthology in the order in which they are initially mentioned in the text.

Now and again, in the need for illustration, or the wish for a particular illustration, I have quoted in the text from a poem that is not in the anthology. Length was naturally a consideration in making decisions about what to include.

I am aware that Browning is not here, and very little Coleridge, and no Dryden, or Spenser, and so little Milton it is a pity. But the anthology is intended to be no more than an introduction to such poems. And the works of all poets, quoted here or not, can be found in any library or bookstore.

Robert Frost's "Bereft," Shakespeare's "O mistress mine," and Byron's "So, We'll Go No More A-Roving" are quoted in their entirety in the text, and are not repeated in the anthology.

POETS REPRESENTED HERE

Sir Philip Sidney (1554–1586)
William Shakespeare (1564–1616)
John Donne (1572–1631)

Robert Herrick (1591–1674)
George Herbert (1593–1633)
John Milton (1608–1674)
Andrew Marvell (1621–1678)
Alexander Pope (1688–1744)
William Blake (1757–1827)
Robert Burns (1759–1796)
William Wordsworth (1770–1850)
Samuel Taylor Coleridge (1772–1834)
George Gordon, Lord Byron (1788–1824)
Percy Bysshe Shelley (1792–1822)
John Keats (1795–1821)
Ralph Waldo Emerson (1803–1882)
Henry Wadsworth Longfellow (1807–1882)
Oliver Wendell Holmes (1809–1894)
Edgar Allan Poe (1809–1849)
Alfred, Lord Tennyson (1809–1892)
Matthew Arnold (1822–1888)
Emily Dickinson (1830–1886)
Gerard Manley Hopkins (1844–1889)
Robert Louis Stevenson (1850–1894)
A. E. Housman (1859–1936)
Robert Frost (1874–1963)
Wilfred Owen (1893–1918)
Edna St. Vincent Millay (1892–1950)
Elizabeth Bishop (1911–1979)
Richard Wilbur (1921–)
Anonymous (seventeenth century)

Loveliest of Trees, the Cherry Now

A. E. Housman

Loveliest of trees, the cherry now
Is hung with bloom along the bough,
And stands about the woodland ride
Wearing white for Eastertide.

Now, of my threescore years and ten,
Twenty will not come again,
And take from seventy springs a score,
It only leaves me fifty more.

And since to look at things in bloom
Fifty springs are little room,
About the woodlands I will go
To see the cherry hung with snow.

The Tuft of Flowers

Robert Frost

I went to turn the grass once after one
Who mowed it in the dew before the sun.

The dew was gone that made his blade so keen
Before I came to view the leveled scene.

I looked for him behind an isle of trees;
I listened for his whetstone on the breeze.

But he had gone his way, the grass all mown,
And I must be, as he had been, — alone,

'As all must be,' I said within my heart,
'Whether they work together or apart.'

But as I said it, swift there passed me by
On noiseless wing a bewildered butterfly,

Seeking with memories grown dim o'er night
Some resting flower of yesterday's delight.

And once I marked his flight go round and round,
As where some flower lay withering on the ground.

And then he flew as far as eye could see,
And then on tremulous wing came back to me.

I thought of questions that have no reply,
And would have turned to toss the grass to dry;

But he turned first, and led my eye to look
At a tall tuft of flowers beside a brook,

A leaping tongue of bloom the scythe had spared
Beside a reedy brook the scythe had bared.

The mower in the dew had loved them thus,
By leaving them to flourish, not for us,

Nor yet to draw one thought of ours to him,
But from sheer morning gladness at the brim.

The butterfly and I had lit upon,
Nevertheless, a message from the dawn,

That made me hear the wakening birds around,
And hear his long scythe whispering to the ground,

And feel a spirit kindred to my own;
So that henceforth I worked no more alone;

But glad with him, I worked as with his aid,
And weary, sought at noon with him the shade;

And dreaming, as it were, held brotherly speech
With one whose thought I had not hoped to reach.

'Men work together,' I told him from the heart,
'Whether they work together or apart.'

A Thing of Beauty (from *Endymion*)

John Keats

A thing of beauty is a joy for ever:
Its loveliness increases; it will never
Pass into nothingness; but still will keep
A bower quiet for us, and a sleep
Full of sweet dreams, and health, and quiet breathing.
Therefore, on every morrow, are we wreathing
A flowery band to bind us to the earth,
Spite of despondence, of the inhuman dearth
Of noble natures, of the gloomy days,
Of all the unhealthy and o'er-darkened ways
Made for our searching: yes, in spite of all,
Some shape of beauty moves away the pall
From our dark spirits. Such the sun, the moon,
Trees old, and young, sprouting a shady boon
For simple sheep, and such are daffodils
With the green world they live in; and clear rills
That for themselves a cooling covert make
'Gainst the hot season; the mid forest brake,
Rich with a sprinkling of fair musk-rose blooms:
And such too is the grandeur of the dooms
We have imagined for the mighty dead;
All lovely tales that we have heard or read:
An endless fountain of immortal drink,
Pouring into us from the heaven's brink.

Nor do we merely feel these essences
For one short hour; no, even as the trees

That whisper round a temple become soon
Dear as the temple's self, so does the moon,
The passion poesy, glories infinite,
Haunt us til they become a cheering light
Unto our souls, and bound to us so fast,
That, whether there be shine, or gloom o'ercast,
They always must be with us, or we die.

Requiem

Robert Louis Stevenson

Under the wide and starry sky
Dig the grave and let me lie.
Glad did I live and gladly die,
  And I laid me down with a will.

This be the verse you grave for me:
Here he lies where he longed to be;
Home is the sailor, home from sea,
  And the hunter home from the hill.

Mending Wall

Robert Frost

Something there is that doesn't love a wall,
That sends the frozen-ground-swell under it,
And spills the upper boulders in the sun;
And makes gaps even two can pass abreast.
The work of hunters is another thing:
I have come after them and made repair
Where they have left not one stone on a stone,
But they would have the rabbit out of hiding,
To please the yelping dogs. The gaps I mean,
No one has seen them made or heard them made,
But at spring mending-time we find them there.
I let my neighbor know beyond the hill;
And on a day we meet to walk the line
And set the wall between us once again.
We keep the wall between us as we go.
To each the boulders that have fallen to each.
And some are loaves and some so nearly balls
We have to use a spell to make them balance:
'Stay where you are until our backs are turned!'
We wear our fingers rough with handling them.
Oh, just another kind of outdoor game,
One on a side. It comes to little more:
There where it is we do not need the wall:
He is all pine and I am apple orchard.
My apple trees will never get across
And eat the cones under his pines, I tell him.

He only says, 'Good fences make good neighbors.'
Spring is the mischief in me, and I wonder
If I could put a notion in his head:
'*Why* do they make good neighbors? Isn't it
Where there are cows? But here there are no cows.
Before I built a wall I'd ask to know
What I was walling in or walling out,
And to whom I was like to give offense.
Something there is that doesn't love a wall,
That wants it down.' I could say 'Elves' to him,
But it's not elves exactly, and I'd rather
He said it for himself. I see him there
Bringing a stone grasped firmly by the top
In each hand, like an old-stone savage armed.
He moves in darkness as it seems to me,
Not of woods only and the shade of trees.
He will not go behind his father's saying,
And he likes having thought of it so well
He says again, 'Good fences make good neighbors.'

From *The Song of Hiawatha*

III. HIAWATHA'S CHILDHOOD

Henry Wadsworth Longfellow

Downward through the evening twilight,
In the days that are forgotten,
In the unremembered ages,
From the full moon fell Nokomis,
Fell the beautiful Nokomis,
   She was a wife, but not a mother.
She was sporting with her women
Swinging in a swing of grapevines,
When her rival, the rejected,
Full of jealousy and hatred,
Cut the leafy swing asunder,
Cut in twain the twisted grapevines,
And Nokomis fell affrighted
Downward through the evening twilight,
On the Muskoday, the meadow,
On the prairie full of blossoms.
"See! a star falls!" said the people;
"From the sky a star is falling!"
There among the ferns and mosses,
There among the prairie lilies,
On the Muskoday, the meadow,
In the moonlight and the starlight,
Fair Nokomis bore a daughter.
And she called her name Wenonah,

As the first-born of her daughters.
And the daughter of Nokomis
Grew up like the prairie lilies,
Grew a tall and slender maiden,
With the beauty of the moonlight,
With the beauty of the starlight.

And Nokomis warned her often,
Saying oft, and oft repeating,
"O, beware of Mudjekeewis,
Of the West-Wind, Mudjekeewis;
Listen not to what he tells you;
Lie not down upon the meadow,
Stoop not down among the lilies,
Lest the West-Wind come and harm you!"

But she heeded not the warning,
Heeded not those words of wisdom,
And the West-Wind came at evening,
Walking lightly o'er the prairie,
Whispering to the leaves and blossoms,
Bending low the flowers and grasses,
Found the beautiful Wenonah,
Lying there among the lilies,
Wooed her with his words of sweetness,
Wooed her with his soft caresses,
Till she bore a son in sorrow,
Bore a son of love and sorrow.

Thus was born my Hiawatha. . . .

From *Macbeth*

ACT 4, SCENE 1

William Shakespeare

All.	Double, double, toil and trouble;
	Fire burn and cauldron bubble.
2nd Witch.	Fillet of a fenny snake,
	In the cauldron boil and bake;
	Eye of newt and toe of frog,
	Wool of bat and tongue of dog,
	Adder's fork and blind-worm's sting,
	Lizard's leg and howlet's wing,
	For a charm of pow'rful trouble,
	Like a hell-broth boil and bubble.
All.	Double, double, toil and trouble;
	Fire burn and cauldron bubble.
3rd Witch.	Scale of dragon, tooth of wolf,
	Witches' mummy, maw and gulf
	Of the ravin'd salt-sea shark,
	Root of hemlock digg'd i' th' dark,
	Liver of blaspheming Jew,
	Gall of goat, and slips of yew
	Sliver'd in the moon's eclipse,
	Nose of Turk and Tartar's lips,
	Finger of birth-strangled babe
	Ditch-deliver'd by a drab,
	Make the gruel thick and slab.

Add thereto a tiger's chauldron.
For th' ingredients of our cauldron.

All.   Double, double, toil and trouble;
Fire burn and cauldron bubble. . . .

"I Wander'd Lonely as a Cloud . . ."

William Wordsworth

I wander'd lonely as a cloud
   That floats on high o'er vales and hills,
When all at once I saw a crowd,
   A host, of golden daffodils;
Beside the lake, beneath the trees,
Fluttering and dancing in the breeze.

Continuous as the stars that shine
   And twinkle on the Milky Way,
They stretched in never-ending line
   Along the margin of a bay:
Ten thousand saw I at a glance,
Tossing their heads in sprightly dance.

The waves beside them danced; but they
   Out-did the sparkling waves in glee:
A poet could not be but gay,
   In such a jocund company:
I gazed — and gazed — but little thought
What wealth the show to me had brought:

For oft, when on my couch I lie
   In vacant or in pensive mood,
They flash upon that inward eye
   Which is the bliss of solitude;
And then my heart with pleasure fills,
And dances with the daffodils.

The World Is Too Much With Us

William Wordsworth

The world is too much with us; late and soon,
   Getting and spending, we lay waste our powers:
   Little we see in Nature that is ours;
We have given our hearts away, a sordid boon!
This sea that bares her bosom to the moon;
   The winds that will be howling at all hours,
   And are up-gather'd now like sleeping flowers;
For this, for everything, we are out of tune;
It moves us not. — Great God! I'd rather be
   A Pagan suckled in a creed outworn;
So might I, standing on this pleasant lea,
   Have glimpses that would make me less forlorn;
Have sight of Proteus rising from the sea;
   Or hear old Triton blow his wreathed horn.

The Destruction of Sennacherib

(from *Hebrew Melodies*)

George Gordon, Lord Byron

I

The Assyrian came down like the wolf on the fold,
And his cohorts were gleaming in purple and gold;
And the sheen of their spears was like stars on the sea,
When the blue wave rolls nightly on deep Galilee.

II

Like the leaves of the forest when Summer is green,
That host with their banners at sunset were seen:
Like the leaves of the forest when Autumn hath blown,
That host on the morrow lay wither'd and strown.

III

For the Angel of Death spread his wings on the blast,
And breathed in the face of the foe as he pass'd;
And the eyes of the sleepers wax'd deadly and chill,
And their hearts but once heaved, and for ever grew still!

IV

And there lay the steed with his nostril all wide,
But through it there roll'd not the breath of his pride;
And the foam of his gasping lay white on the turf,
And cold as the spray of the rock-beating surf.

V

And there lay the rider distorted and pale,
With the dew on his brow, and the rust on his mail:
And the tents were all silent, the banners alone,
The lances unlifted, the trumpet unblown.

VI

And the widows of Ashur are loud in their wail,
And the idols are broke in the temple of Baal;
And the might of the Gentile, unsmote by the sword,
Hath melted like snow in the glance of the Lord!

Sonnet 18

William Shakespeare

Shall I compare thee to a summer's day?
Thou art more lovely and more temperate.
Rough winds do shake the darling buds of May,
And summer's lease hath all too short a date;
Sometimes too hot the eye of heaven shines,
And often is his gold complexion dimm'd;
And every fair from fair sometimes declines,
By chance or nature's changing course untrimm'd:
But thy eternal summer shall not fade
Nor lose possession of that fair thou ow'st;
Nor shall Death brag thou wand'rest in his shade,
When in eternal lines to time thou grow'st;
    So long as men can breathe or eyes can see,
    So long lives this, and this gives life to thee.

Sonnet 29

William Shakespeare

When, in disgrace with Fortune and men's eyes,
I all alone beweep my outcast state,
And trouble deaf heaven with my bootless cries,
And look upon myself and curse my fate,
Wishing me like to one more rich in hope,
Featured like him, like him with friends possess'd,
Desiring this man's art, and that man's scope,
With what I most enjoyed contented least;
Yet in these thoughts myself almost despising,
Haply I think on thee; and then my state,
Like to the lark at break of day arising
From sullen earth, sings hymns at heaven's gate;
   For thy sweet love rememb'red such wealth brings
   That then I scorn to change my state with kings.

On the Grasshopper and the Cricket

John Keats

The poetry of earth is never dead:
　　When all the birds are faint with the hot sun,
　　And hide in cooling trees, a voice will run
From hedge to hedge about the new-mown mead;
That is the Grasshopper's — he takes the lead
　　In summer luxury, — he has never done
　　With his delights; for when tired out with fun
He rests at ease beneath some pleasant weed.
The poetry of earth is ceasing never:
　　On a lone winter evening, when the frost
　　　Has wrought a silence, from the stove there shrills
The Cricket's song, in warmth increasing ever,
　　And seems to one in drowsiness half lost,
　　　The Grasshopper's among some grassy hills.

To His Coy Mistress

Andrew Marvell

Had we but world enough, and time,
This coyness, Lady, were no crime.
We would sit down and think which way
To walk and pass our long love's day.
Thou by the Indian Ganges' side
Shouldst rubies find: I by the tide
of Humber would complain. I would
Love you ten years before the Flood,
And you should, if you please, refuse
Till the conversion of the Jews.
My vegetable love should grow
Vaster than empires, and more slow;
An hundred years should go to praise
Thine eyes and on thy forehead gaze;
Two hundred to adore each breast;
But thirty thousand to the rest;
An age at least to every part,
And the last age should show your heart;
For, Lady, you deserve this state,
Nor would I love at lower rate.

But at my back I always hear
Time's wingèd chariot hurrying near;
And yonder all before us lie
Deserts of vast eternity.
Thy beauty shall no more be found,
Nor, in thy marble vault, shall sound

My echoing song: then worms shall try
That long preserved virginity,
And your quaint honour turn to dust,
And into ashes all my lust:
The grave's a fine and private place,
But none, I think, do there embrace.
 Now therefore, while the youthful hue
Sits on thy skin like morning dew,
And while thy willing soul transpires
At every pore with instant fires,
Now let us sport us while we may,
And now, like amorous birds of prey,
Rather at once our time devour
Than languish in his slow-chapt power.
Let us roll all our strength and all
Our sweetness up into one ball,
And tear our pleasures with rough strife
Through the iron gates of life:
Thus, though we cannot make our sun
Stand still, yet we will make him run.

Delight in Disorder

Robert Herrick

A sweet disorder in the dress
Kindles in clothes a wantonness:
A lawn about the shoulders thrown
Into a fine distraction:
An erring lace, which here and there
Enthrals the crimson stomacher:
A cuff neglectful, and thereby
Ribbands to flow confusedly:
A winning wave, deserving note,
In the tempestuous petticoat:
A careless shoe-string, in whose tie
I see a wild civility:
Do more bewitch me than when art
Is too precise in every part.

The Tyger

William Blake

Tyger! Tyger! burning bright
In the forests of the night,
What immortal hand or eye
Could frame thy fearful symmetry?

In what distant deeps or skies
Burnt the fire of thine eyes?
On what wings dare he aspire?
What the hand dare seize the fire?

And what shoulder, and what art,
Could twist the sinews of thy heart?
And when thy heart began to beat,
What dread hand? and what dread feet?

What the hammer? what the chain?
In what furnace was thy brain?
What the anvil? what dread grasp
Dare its deadly terrors clasp?

When the stars threw down their spears,
And water'd heaven with their tears,
Did he smile his work to see?
Did he who made the Lamb make thee?

Tyger! Tyger! burning bright
In the forests of the night,
What immortal hand or eye,
Dare frame thy fearful symmetry?

Moriturus

Edna St. Vincent Millay

If I could have
   Two things in one:
The peace of the grave,
   And the light of the sun;

My hands across
   My thin breast-bone,
But aware of the moss
   Invading the stone,

Aware of the flight
   Of the golden flicker
With his wing to the light;
   To hear him nicker

And drum with his bill
   On the rotted willow;
Snug and still
   On a grey pillow

Deep in the clay
   Where digging is hard,
Out of the way, —
   The blue shard

Of a broken platter —
   If I might be
Insensate matter
   With sensate me

Sitting within,
   Harking and prying,
I might begin
   To dicker with dying.

For the body at best
   Is a bundle of aches,
Longing for rest;
   It cries when it wakes

"Alas, 'tis light!"
   At set of sun
"Alas, 'tis night,
   And nothing done!"

Death, however,
   Is a spongy wall,
Is a sticky river,
   Is nothing at all.

Summon the weeper,
   Wail and sing;
Call him Reaper,
   Angel, King;

Call him Evil
   Drunk to the lees,
Monster, Devil, —
   He is less than these.

Call him Thief,
   The Maggot in the Cheese,
The Canker in the Leaf, —
   He is less than these.

Dusk without sound,
     Where the spirit by pain
Uncoiled, is wound
     To spring again;

The mind enmeshed
     Laid straight in repose,
And the body refreshed
     By feeding the rose, —

These are but visions;
     These would be
The grave's derisions,
     Could the grave see.

Here is the wish
     Of one that died
Like a beached fish
     On the ebb of the tide:

That he might wait
     Till the tide came back,
To see if a crate,
     Or a bottle, or a black

Boot, or an oar,
     Or an orange peel
Be washed ashore. . . .
     About his heel

The sand slips;
     The last he hears
From the world's lips
     Is the sand in his ears.

What thing is little? —
   The aphis hid
In a house of spittle?
   The hinge of the lid

Of the spider's eye
   At the spider's birth?
"Greater am I
   By the earth's girth

Than Mighty Death!"
   All creatures cry
That can summon breath; —
   And speak no lie.

For He is nothing;
   He is less
Than Echo answering
   "Nothingness!" —

Less than the heat
   Of the furthest star
To the ripening wheat;
   Less by far,

When all the lipping
   Is said and sung,
Than the sweat dripping
   From a dog's tongue.

This being so,
   And I being such,
I would liever go
   On a cripple's crutch,

Lopped and felled;
  Liever be dependent
On a chair propelled
  By a surly attendant

With a foul breath,
  And be spooned my food,
Than go with Death
  Where nothing good,

Not even the thrust
  Of the summer gnat,
Consoles the dust
  For being that.

Needy, lonely,
  Stitched by pain,
Left with only
  The drip of the rain

Out of all I had;
  The books of the wise,
Badly read
  By other eyes,

Lewdly bawled
  At my closing ear;
Hated, called
  A lingerer here; —

Withstanding Death
  Till Life be gone,
I shall treasure my breath,
  I shall linger on.

I shall bolt my door
  With a bolt and a cable;
I shall block my door
  With a bureau and a table;

With all my might
  My door shall be barred.
I shall put up a fight,
  I shall take it hard.

With his hand on my mouth
  He shall drag me forth,
Shrieking to the south
  And clutching at the north.

From *A Midsummer Night's Dream*

ACT 2, SCENE 2

William Shakespeare

Oberon.

> I know a bank where the wild thyme blows,
> Where oxlips and the nodding violet grows,
> Quite over-canopi'd with luscious woodbine,
> With sweet musk-roses and with eglantine.
> There sleeps Titania sometime of the night,
> Lull'd in these flowers with dances and delight;
> And there the snake throws her enamell'd skin,
> Weed wide enough to wrap a fairy in;
> And with the juice of this I'll streak her eyes,
> And make her full of hateful fantasies.

From *Paradise Lost,* Book II

John Milton

But now at last the sacred influence
Of light appears, and from the walls of Heav'n
Shoots farr into the bosom of dim Night
A glimmering dawn; here Nature first begins
Her fardest verge, and *Chaos* to retire
As from her outmost works a brok'n foe
With tumult less and with less hostile din,
That *Satan* with less toil, and now with ease
Wafts on the calmer wave by dubious light
And like a weather-beaten Vessel holds
Gladly the Port, though Shrouds and Tackle torn;
Or in the emptier waste, resembling Air,
Weighs his spread wings, at leasure to behold
Farr off th' Empyreal Heav'n, extended wide
In circuit, undetermined square or round,
With Opal Towrs and Battlements adorn'd
Of living Saphire, once his native Seat;
And fast by hanging in a golden Chain
This pendant world, in bigness as a Starr
Of smallest Magnitude close by the Moon.
Thither full fraught with mischievous revenge,
Accurst, and in a cursed hour he hies.

Ozymandias

Percy Bysshe Shelley

I met a traveller from an antique land
Who said: Two vast and trunkless legs of stone
Stand in the desert . . . Near them, on the sand,
Half sunk, a shattered visage lies, whose frown,
And wrinkled lip, and sneer of cold command,
Tell that its sculptor well those passions read
Which yet survive, stamped on these lifeless things,
The hand that mocked them, and the heart that fed:
And on the pedestal these words appear:
'My name is Ozymandias, king of kings:
Look on my works, ye Mighty, and despair!'
Nothing beside remains. Round the decay
Of that colossal wreck, boundless and bare
The lone and level sands stretch far away.

Sonnet 87

William Shakespeare

Farewell! thou art too dear for my possessing,
And like enough thou know'st thy estimate.
The charter of thy worth gives thee releasing;
My bonds in thee are all determinate.
For how do I hold thee but by thy granting,
And for that riches where is my deserving?
The cause of this fair gift in me is wanting,
And so my patent back again is swerving.
Thyself thou gav'st, thy own worth then not knowing,
Or me, to whom thou gav'st it, else mistaking;
So thy great gift, upon misprision growing,
Comes home again, on better judgment making.
    Thus have I had thee as a dream doth flatter —
    In sleep a king, but waking no such matter.

Sonnet
Written on a Blank Page in Shakespeare's Poems, facing "A Lover's Complaint."

John Keats

Bright star, would I were stedfast as thou art —
　Not in lone splendour hung aloft the night
And watching, with eternal lids apart,
　Like nature's patient, sleepless Eremite,
The moving waters at their priestlike task
　Of pure ablution round earth's human shores,
Or gazing on the new soft-fallen mask
　Of snow upon the mountains and the moors —
No — yet still stedfast, still unchangeable,
　Pillow'd upon my fair love's ripening breast,
To feel for ever its soft fall and swell,
　Awake for ever in a sweet unrest,
Still, still to hear her tender-taken breath,
And so live ever — or else swoon to death.

Astrophel and Stella

SONNET 39

Sir Philip Sidney

Come, Sleep; O Sleep! the certain knot of peace,
The baiting-place of wit, the balm of woe,
The poor man's wealth, the prisoner's release,
Th' indifferent judge between the high and low;
With shield of proof shield me from out the prease
Of those fierce darts Despair at me doth throw:
O make in me those civil wars to cease;
I will good tribute pay, if thou do so.
Take thou of me smooth pillows, sweetest bed,
A chamber deaf to noise and blind of light,
A rosy garland and a weary head;
And if these things, as being thine in right,
   Move not thy heavy grace, thou shalt in me,
   Livelier than elsewhere, Stella's image see.

Stopping by Woods on a Snowy Evening

Robert Frost

Whose woods these are I think I know.
His house is in the village though;
He will not see me stopping here
To watch his woods fill up with snow.

My little horse must think it queer
To stop without a farmhouse near
Between the woods and frozen lake
The darkest evening of the year.

He gives his harness bells a shake
To ask if there is some mistake.
The only other sound's the sweep
Of easy wind and downy flake.

The woods are lovely, dark and deep,
But I have promises to keep,
And miles to go before I sleep,
And miles to go before I sleep.

The Wife of Usher's Well

Anonymous

There lived a wife at Usher's well,
    And a wealthy wife was she;
She had three stout and stalwart sons,
    And sent them o'er the sea.

They hadna been a week from her,
    A week but barely ane,
When word came to the carline wife
    That her three sons were gane.

They hadna been a week from her,
    A week but barely three,
When word came to the carline wife
    That her sons she'd never see.

"I wish the wind may never cease,
    Nor fashes in the flood,
Till my three sons come hame to me,
    In earthly flesh and blood!"

It fell about the Martinmas,
    When nights are lang and mirk,
The carline wife's three sons came hame,
    And their hats were o' the birk.

It neither grew in syke nor ditch,
    Nor yet in ony sheugh;
But at the gates o' Paradise
    That birk grew fair eneugh.

---

carline = country   *fashes* = troubles   *syke* = marsh   *sheugh* = trench

"Blow up the fire, my maidens!
        Bring water from the well!
For a' my house shall feast this night,
        Since my three sons are well."

And she has made to them a bed,
        She's made it large and wide;
And she's ta'en her mantle her about,
        Sat down at the bedside.

Up then crew the red, red cock,
        And up and crew the gray;
The eldest to the youngest said,
        "'Tis time we were away."

The cock he hadna craw'd but once,
        And clapp'd his wings at a',
When the youngest to the eldest said,
        "Brother, we must awa'."

"The cock doth craw, the day doth daw,
        The channerin' worm doth chide;
Gin we be miss'd out o' our place,
        A sair pain we maun bide."

"Lie still, lie still but a little wee while,
        Lie still but if we may;
Gin my mother should miss us when she wakes,
        She'll go mad ere it be day."

"Fare ye weel, my mother dear!
        Fareweel to barn and byre!
And fare ye weel, the bonny lass
        That kindles my mother's fire!"

----

channerin' = fretting

I died for Beauty — but was scarce

Emily Dickinson

I died for Beauty — but was scarce
Adjusted in the Tomb
When One who died for Truth, was lain
In an adjoining Room —

He questioned softly "Why I failed"?
"For Beauty", I replied —
"And I — for Truth — Themself are One —
We Bretheren, are", He said —

And so, as Kinsmen, met a Night —
We talked between the Rooms —
Until the Moss had reached our lips —
And covered up — our names —

From *"An Essay on Criticism"*

Alexander Pope

Expression is the dress of thought, and still
Appears more decent as more suitable;
A vile conceit in pompous words expressed,
Is like a clown in regal purple dressed;
For different styles with different subjects sort,
As several garbs with country, town, and court.
Some by old words to fame have made pretence;
Ancients in phrase, mere moderns in their sense!
Such laboured nothings, in so strange a style,
Amaze the unlearned, and make the learnèd smile.
Unlucky, as Fungoso in the play,
These sparks with awkward vanity display
What the fine gentleman wore yesterday;
And but so mimic ancient wits at best,
As apes our grandsires in their doublets drest.
In words, as fashions, the same rule will hold;
Alike fantastic, if too new, or old;
But not the first by whom the new are tried,
Nor yet the last to lay the old aside.
　　But most by *numbers* judge a poet's song,
And smooth or rough, with them, is right or wrong;
In the bright Muse though thousand charms conspire,
Her voice is all these tuneful fools admire,
Who haunt Parnassus but to please their ear,
Not mend their minds; as some to church repair,
Not for the doctrine but the music there.

These equal syllables alone require,
Though oft the ear the open vowels tire,
While expletives their feeble aid do join,
And ten low words oft creep in one dull line,
While they ring round the same unvaried chimes,
With sure returns of still expected rhymes.
Where'er you find 'the cooling western breeze,'
In the next line, it 'whispers through the trees';
If crystal streams 'with pleasing murmurs creep,'
The reader's threatened (not in vain) with 'sleep.'
Then, at the last and only couplet fraught
With some unmeaning thing they call a thought,
A needless Alexandrine ends the song,
That, like a wounded snake, drags its slow length along.
Leave such to tune their own dull rhymes, and know
What's roundly smooth, or languishingly slow;
And praise the easy vigour of a line
Where Denham's strength, and Waller's sweetness join.
True ease in writing comes from art, not chance,
As those move easiest who have learned to dance.
'Tis not enough no harshness gives offence,
The sound must seem an echo to the sense.
Soft is the strain when Zephyr gently blows,
And the smooth stream in smoother numbers flows;
But when loud surges lash the sounding shore,
The hoarse, rough verse should like the torrent roar.

Annabel Lee

Edgar Allan Poe

It was many and many a year ago,
  In a kingdom by the sea,
That a maiden there lived whom you may know
  By the name of Annabel Lee; —
And this maiden she lived with no other thought
  Than to love and be loved by me.

She was a child and *I* was a child,
  In this kingdom by the sea,
But we loved with a love that was more than love —
  I and my Annabel Lee —
With a love that the wingéd seraphs of Heaven
  Coveted her and me.

And this was the reason that, long ago,
  In this kingdom by the sea,
A wind blew out of a cloud by night
  Chilling my Annabel Lee;
So that her highborn kinsmen came
  And bore her away from me,
To shut her up in a sepulchre
  In this kingdom by the sea.

The angels, not half so happy in Heaven,
  Went envying her and me: —
Yes! that was the reason (as all men know,
  In this kingdom by the sea)

That the wind came out of the cloud, chilling
    And killing my Annabel Lee.

But our love it was stronger by far than the love
    Of those who were older than we —
    Of many far wiser than we —
And neither the angels in Heaven above
    Nor the demons down under the sea
Can ever dissever my soul from the soul
    Of the beautiful Annabel Lee: —

For the moon never beams without bringing me dreams
    Of the beautiful Annabel Lee;
And the stars never rise but I see the bright eyes
    Of the beautiful Annabel Lee;
And so, all the night-tide, I lie down by the side
Of my darling, my darling, my life and my bride
    In her sepulchre there by the sea —
    In her tomb by the side of the sea.

Stanzas Written on the Road Between Florence and Pisa

George Gordon, Lord Byron

Oh, talk not to me of a name great in story;
The days of our youth are the days of our glory;
And the myrtle and ivy of sweet two-and-twenty
Are worth all your laurels, though ever so plenty.

What are garlands and crowns to the brow that is wrinkled?
'Tis but as a dead flower with May-dew be-sprinkled:
Then away with all such from the head that is hoary!
What care I for the wreaths that can *only* give glory?

Oh Fame! — if I e'er took delight in thy praises,
'Twas less for the sake of thy high-sounding phrases,
Than to see the bright eyes of the dear one discover
She thought that I was not unworthy to love her.

There chiefly I sought thee, *there* only I found thee;
Her glance was the best of the rays that surround thee;
When it sparkled o'er aught that was bright in my story,
I knew it was love, and I felt it was glory.

The Chambered Nautilus

Oliver Wendell Holmes

This is the ship of pearl, which, poets feign,
   Sails the unshadowed main, —
   The venturous bark that flings
On the sweet summer wind its purpled wings
In gulfs enchanted, where the Siren sings,
   And coral reefs lie bare,
Where the cold sea-maids rise to sun their streaming hair.

Its webs of living gauze no more unfurl;
   Wrecked is the ship of pearl!
   And every chambered cell,
Where its dim dreaming of life was wont to dwell,
As the frail tenant shaped his growing shell,
   Before thee lies revealed, —
Its irised ceiling rent, its sunless crypt unsealed!

Year after year beheld the silent toil
   That spread his lustrous coil;
   Still, as the spiral grew,
He left the past year's dwelling for the new,
Stole with soft step its shining archway through,
   Built up its idle door,
Stretched in his last-found home, and knew the old no
     more.

Thanks for the heavenly message brought by thee,
   Child of the wandering sea,
   Cast from her lap, forlorn!

From thy dead lips a clearer note is born
Than ever Triton blew from wreathèd horn!
    While on mine ear it rings,
Through the deep caves of thought I hear a voice that
        sings: —

Build thee more stately mansions, O my soul,
    As the swift seasons roll!
    Leave thy low-vaulted past!
Let each new temple, nobler than the last,
Shut thee from heaven with a dome more vast,
    Till thou at length art free,
Leaving thine outgrown shell by life's unresting sea!

Arms and the Boy

Wilfred Owen

Let the boy try along this bayonet-blade
How cold steel is, and keen with hunger of blood;
Blue with all malice, like a madman's flash;
And thinly drawn with famishing for flesh.

Lend him to stroke these blind, blunt bullet-leads
Which long to nuzzle in the hearts of lads,
Or give him cartridges of fine zinc teeth,
Sharp with the sharpness of grief and death.

For his teeth seem for laughing round an apple.
There lurk no claws behind his fingers supple;
And god will grow no talons at his heels,
Nor antlers through the thickness of his curls.

The Rhodora:

ON BEING ASKED, WHENCE IS THE FLOWER?

Ralph Waldo Emerson

In May, when sea-winds pierced our solitudes,
I found the fresh Rhodora in the woods,
Spreading its leafless blooms in a damp nook,
To please the desert and the sluggish brook.
The purple petals, fallen in the pool,
Made the black water with their beauty gay;
Here might the red-bird come his plumes to cool,
And court the flower that cheapens his array.
Rhodora! if the sages ask thee why
This charm is wasted on the earth and sky,
Tell them, dear, that if eyes were made for seeing,
Then Beauty is its own excuse for being:
Why thou were there, O rival of the rose!
I never thought to ask, I never knew:
But, in my simple ignorance, suppose
The self-same Power that brought me there brought you.

Ode to the West Wind

Percy Bysshe Shelley

I

O Wild West wind, thou breath of Autumn's being,
Thou, from whose unseen presence the leaves dead
Are driven, like ghosts from an enchanter fleeing,

Yellow, and black, and pale, and hectic red,
Pestilence-stricken multitudes: O thou,
Who chariotest to their dark wintry bed

The wingèd seeds, where they lie cold and low,
Each like a corpse within its grave, until
Thine azure sister of the Spring shall blow

Her clarion o'er the dreaming earth, and fill
(Driving sweet buds like flocks to feed in air)
With living hues and odours plain and hill:

Wild Spirit, which art moving everywhere;
Destroyer and preserver; hear, oh, hear!

II

Thou on whose stream, mid the steep sky's commotion,
Loose clouds like earth's decaying leaves are shed,
Shook from the tangled boughs of Heaven and Ocean,

Angels of rain and lightning: there are spread
On the blue surface of thine aëry surge,
Like the bright hair uplifted from the head

Of some fierce Maenad, even from the dim verge
Of the horizon to the zenith's height,
The locks of the approaching storm. Thou dirge

Of the dying year, to which this closing night
Will be the dome of a vast sepulchre,
Vaulted with all thy congregated might

Of vapours, from whose solid atmosphere
Black rain, and fire, and hail will burst: oh, hear!

III

Thou, who didst waken from his summer dreams
The blue Mediterranean, where he lay,
Lulled by the coil of his crystàlline streams,

Beside a pumice isle in Baiae's bay,
And saw in sleep old palaces and towers
Quivering within the wave's intenser day,

All overgrown with azure moss and flowers
So sweet, the sense faints picturing them! Thou
For whose path the Atlantic's level powers

Cleave themselves into chasms, while far below
The sea-blooms and the oozy woods which wear
The sapless foliage of the ocean, know

Thy voice, and suddenly grow gray with fear,
And tremble and despoil themselves: oh, hear!

IV

If I were a dead leaf thou mightest bear;
If I were a swift cloud to fly with thee;
A wave to pant beneath thy power, and share

The impulse of thy strength, only less free
Than thou, O uncontrollable! If even
I were as in my boyhood, and could be

The comrade of thy wanderings over Heaven,
As then, when to outstrip thy skiey speed
Scare seemed a vision; I would ne'er have striven

As thus with thee in prayer in my sore need.
Oh, lift me as a wave, a leaf, a cloud!
I fall upon the thorns of life! I bleed!

A heavy weight of hours has chained and bowed
One too like thee: tameless, and swift, and proud.

v

Make me thy lyre, even as the forest is:
What if my leaves are falling like its own!
The tumult of thy mighty harmonies

Will take from both a deep, autumnal tone,
Sweet though in sadness. Be thou, Spirit fierce,
My spirit! Be thou me, impetuous one!

Drive my dead thoughts over the universe
Like withered leaves to quicken a new birth!
And, by the incantation of this verse,

Scatter, as from an unextinguished hearth
Ashes and sparks, my words among mankind!
Be through my lips to unawakened earth

The trumpet of a prophecy! O, Wind,
If Winter comes, can Spring be far behind?

A Red, Red Rose

Robert Burns

O my Luve's like a red, red rose,
    That's newly sprung in June:
O my Luve's like the melodie
    That's sweetly played in tune!

As fair art thou, my bonnie lass,
    So deep in luve am I:
And I will luve thee still, my dear,
    Till a' the seas gang dry:

Till a' the seas gang dry, my dear,
    And the rocks melt wi' the sun;
I will luve thee still, my dear,
    While the sands o' life shall run.

And fare thee weel, my only Luve!
    And fare thee weel a while!
And I will come again, my Luve,
    Tho' it were ten thousand mile!

Requiscat

Matthew Arnold

Strew on her roses, roses,
   And never a spray of yew.
In quiet she reposes:
   Ah! would that I did too.

Her mirth the world required:
   She bathed it in smiles of glee.
But her heart was tired, tired,
   And now they let her be.

Her life was turning, turning,
   In mazes of heat and sound.
But for peace her soul was yearning,
   And now peace laps her round.

Her cabin'd, ample Spirit,
   It flutter'd and fail'd for breath.
To-night it doth inherit
   The vasty hall of Death.

Eight O'Clock

A. E. Housman

He stood, and heard the steeple
  Sprinkle the quarters on the morning town.
One, two, three, four, to market-place and people
  It tossed them down.

Strapped, noosed, nighing his hour,
  He stood and counted them and cursed his luck;
And then the clock collected in the tower
  Its strength, and struck.

From *In Memoriam*

Alfred, Lord Tennyson

LIII

Oh yet we trust that somehow good
  Will be the final goal of ill,
  To pangs of nature, sins of will,
Defects of doubt, and taints of blood;

That nothing walks with aimless feet;
  That not one life shall be destroy'd,
  Or cast as rubbish to the void,
When God hath made the pile complete;

That not a worm is cloven in vain;
  That not a moth with vain desire
  Is shrivel'd in a fruitless fire,
Or but subserves another's gain.

Behold, we know not anything;
  I can but trust that good shall fall
  At last — far off — at last, to all,
And every winter change to spring.

So runs my dream: but what am I?
  An infant crying in the night:
  An infant crying for the light:
And with no language but a cry.

From *Romeo and Juliet*

ACT 1, SCENE 5

William Shakespeare

Romeo. If I profane with my unworthiest hand
   This holy shrine, the gentle sin is this:
My lips, two blushing pilgrims, ready stand
   To smooth that rough touch with a tender kiss.

Juliet. Good pilgrim, you do wrong your hand too much,
   Which mannerly devotion shows in this;
For saints have hands that pilgrims' hands do touch,
   And palm to palm is holy palmers' kiss.

Romeo. Have not saints lips, and holy palmers too?

Juliet. Ay, pilgrim, lips that they must use in prayer.

Romeo. O, then, dear saint, let lips do what hands do;
   They pray; grant thou, lest faith turn to despair.

Juliet. Saints do not move, though grant for prayers' sake.

Romeo. Then move not while my prayer's effect I take.
   Thus from my lips, by thine my sin is purg'd.
                    [*Kissing her.*]

The Eagle

Alfred, Lord Tennyson

He clasps the crag with crooked hands;
Close to the sun in lonely lands,
Ring'd with the azure world, he stands.

The wrinkled sea beneath him crawls;
He watches from his mountain walls,
And like a thunderbolt he falls.

One Art

Elizabeth Bishop

The art of losing isn't hard to master;
so many things seem filled with the intent
to be lost that their loss is no disaster.

Lose something every day. Accept the fluster
of lost door keys, the hour badly spent.
The art of losing isn't hard to master.

Then practice losing farther, losing faster:
places, and names, and where it was you meant
to travel. None of these will bring disaster.

I lost my mother's watch. And look! my last, or
next-to-last, of three loved houses went.
The art of losing isn't hard to master.

I lost two cities, lovely ones. And, vaster,
some realms I owned, two rivers, a continent.
I miss them, but it wasn't a disaster.

— Even losing you (the joking voice, a gesture
I love) I shan't have lied. It's evident
the art of losing's not too hard to master
though it may look like (*Write* it!) like disaster.

Song

John Donne

Go and catch a falling star,
  Get with child a mandrake root,
Tell me where all past years are,
  Or who cleft the Devil's foot;
Teach me to hear mermaids singing,
  Or to keep off envy's stinging,
      And find
      What wind
Serves to advance an honest mind.

If thou be'st born to strange sights,
  Things invisible to see,
Ride ten thousand days and nights
  Till Age snow white hairs on thee;
Thou, when thou return'st, wilt tell me
All strange wonders that befell thee,
      And swear
      No where
Lives a woman true and fair.

If thou find'st one, let me know;
  Such a pilgrimage were sweet.
Yet do not; I would not go,
  Though at next door we might meet.
Though she were true when you met her,

And last till you write your letter,
      Yet she
      Will be
False, ere I come, to two or three.

The Flower

George Herbert

How fresh, O Lord, how sweet and clean
Are thy returns! ev'n as the flowers in spring;
   To which, besides their own demean,
The late-past frosts tributes of pleasure bring.
      Grief melts away
      Like snow in May,
As if there were no such cold thing.

Who would have thought my shrivelled heart
Could have recovered greenness? It was gone
   Quite underground; as flowers depart
To see their mother-root, when they have blown;
      Where they together
      All the hard weather,
Dead to the world, keep house unknown.

These are thy wonders, Lord of power,
Killing and quick'ning, bringing down to hell
   And up to heaven in an hour;
Making a chiming of a passing-bell.
      We say amiss,
      This or that is:
Thy word is all, if we could spell.

O that I once past changing were,
Fast in thy Paradise, where no flower can wither!
   Many a spring I shoot up fair,

Off'ring at heav'n, growing and groaning thither:
    Nor doth my flower
    Want a spring-shower,
My sins and I joining together:

But while I grow in a straight line,
Still upwards bent, as if heav'n were mine own,
    Thy anger comes, and I decline:
What frost to that? what pole is not the zone,
    Where all things burn,
    When thou dost turn,
And the least frown of thine is shown?

And now in age I bud again,
After so many deaths I live and write;
    I once more smell the dew and rain,
And relish versing: O my only light,
    It cannot be
    That I am he
On whom thy tempests fell all night.

These are thy wonders, Lord of love,
To make us see we are but flowers that glide:
    Which when we once can find and prove,
Thou hast a garden for us, where to bide.
    Who would be more,
    Swelling through store,
Forfeit their Paradise by their pride.

Kubla Khan

Samuel Taylor Coleridge

In Xanadu did Kubla Khan
A stately pleasure-dome decree:
Where Alph, the sacred river, ran
Through caverns measureless to man
   Down to a sunless sea.
So twice five miles of fertile ground
With walls and towers are girdled round:
And there were gardens bright with sinuous rills,
Where blossomed many an incense-bearing tree;
And here were forests ancient as the hills,
Enfolding sunny spots of greenery.

But oh! that deep romantic chasm which slanted
Down the green hill athwart a cedarn cover!
A savage place! as holy and enchanted
As e'er beneath a waning moon was haunted
By woman wailing for her demon-lover!
And from this chasm, with ceaseless turmoil seething,
As if this earth in fast thick pants were breathing,
A mighty fountain momently was forced:
Amid whose swift half-intermitted burst
Huge fragments vaulted like rebounding hail,
Or chaffy grain beneath the thresher's flail:
And 'mid these dancing rocks at once and ever
It flung up momently the sacred river.
Five miles meandering with a mazy motion
Through wood and dale the sacred river ran,

Then reached the caverns measureless to man,
And sank in tumult to a lifeless ocean:
And 'mid this tumult Kubla heard from far
Ancestral voices prophesying war!
    The shadow of the dome of pleasure
    Floated midway on the waves;
    Where was heard the mingled measure
    From the fountain and the caves.
It was a miracle of rare device,
A sunny pleasure-dome with caves of ice!

    A damsel with a dulcimer
    In a vision once I saw:
    It was an Abyssinian maid,
    And on her dulcimer she played,
    Singing of Mount Abora.
    Could I revive within me
    Her symphony and song,
    To such a deep delight 'twould win me,
That with music loud and long,
I would build that dome in air,
That sunny dome! those caves of ice!
And all who heard should see them there,
And all should cry, Beware! Beware!
His flashing eyes, his floating hair!
Weave a circle round him thrice,
And close your eyes with holy dread,
For he on honey-dew hath fed,
And drunk the milk of Paradise.

To a Skylark

Percy Bysshe Shelley

Hail to thee, blithe Spirit!
   Bird thou never wert,
That from Heaven, or near it,
   Pourest thy full heart
In profuse strains of unpremeditated art.

   Higher still and higher
     From the earth thou springest
Like a cloud of fire;
     The blue deep thou wingest,
And singing still dost soar, and soaring ever singest.

   In the golden lightning
     Of the sunken sun,
O'er which clouds are bright'ning,
     Thou dost float and run;
Like an unbodied joy whose race is just begun.

   The pale purple even
     Melts around thy flight;
Like a star of Heaven,
     In the broad daylight
Thou art unseen, but yet I hear thy shrill delight.

   Keen as are the arrows
     Of that silver sphere,
Whose intense lamp narrows
     In the white dawn clear,
Until we hardly see — we feel that it is there.

All the earth and air
  With thy voice is loud,
As, when night is bare,
  From one lonely cloud
The moon rains out her beams, and Heaven is overflowed.

What thou art we know not;
  What is most like thee?
From rainbow clouds there flow not
  Drops so bright to see,
As from thy presence showers a rain of melody.

Like a Poet hidden
  In the light of thought,
Singing hymns unbidden,
  Till the world is wrought
To sympathy with hopes and fears it heeded not:

Like a high-born maiden
  In a palace-tower,
Soothing her love-laden
  Soul in secret hour
With music sweet as love, which overflows her bower:

Like a glow-worm golden
  In a dell of dew,
Scattering unbeholden
  Its aëreal hue
Among the flowers and grass, which screen it from the view!

Like a rose embowered
  In its own green leaves,
By warm winds deflowered,
  Till the scent it gives
Makes faint with too much sweet those heavy-wingèd thieves.

Sound of vernal showers
    On the twinkling grass,
Rain-awakened flowers,
    All that ever was
Joyous, and clear, and fresh, thy music doth surpass.

    Teach us, Sprite or Bird,
        What sweet thoughts are thine:
    I have never heard
        Praise of love or wine
That panted forth a flood of rapture so divine.

    Chorus Hymeneal,
        Or triumphal chant,
    Matched with thine would be all
        But an empty vaunt,
A thing wherein we feel there is some hidden want.

    What objects are the fountains
        Of thy happy strain?
    What fields, or waves, or mountains?
        What shapes of sky or plain?
What love of thine own kind? what ignorance of pain?

    With thy clear keen joyance
        Languor cannot be:
    Shadow of annoyance
        Never came near thee:
Thou lovest — but ne'er knew love's sad satiety.

    Waking or asleep,
        Thou of death must deem
    Things more true and deep
        Than we mortals dream,
Or how could thy notes flow in such a crystal stream?

We look before and after,
    And pine for what is not:
Our sincerest laughter
    With some pain is fraught;
Our sweetest songs are those that tell of saddest thought.

Yet if we could scorn
    Hate, and pride, and fear;
If we were things born
    Not to shed a tear,
I know not how thy joy we ever should come near.

Better than all measures
    Of delightful sound,
Better than all treasures
    That in books are found,
Thy skill to poet were, thou scorner of the ground!

Teach me half the gladness
    That thy brain must know,
Such harmonious madness
    From my lips would flow,
The world should listen then — as I am listening now.

Parable

Richard Wilbur

I read how Quixote in his random ride
Came to a crossing once, and lest he lose
The purity of chance, would not decide

Whither to fare, but wished his horse to choose.
For glory lay wherever he might turn.
His head was light with pride, his horse's shoes

Were heavy, and he headed for the barn.

God's Grandeur

Gerard Manley Hopkins

The world is charged with the grandeur of God.
　　It will flame out, like shining from shook foil;
　　It gathers to a greatness, like the ooze of oil
Crushed. Why do men then now not reck his rod?
Generations have trod, have trod, have trod;
　　And all is seared with trade; bleared, smeared with toil;
　　And wears man's smudge and shares man's smell: the soil
Is bare now, nor can foot feel, being shod.

And for all this, nature is never spent;
　　There lives the dearest freshness deep down things;
And though the last lights off the black West went
　　Oh, morning, at the brown brink eastward, springs —
Because the Holy Ghost over the bent
　　World broods with warm breast and with ah! bright wings.

Ode to a Nightingale

John Keats

I

My heart aches, and a drowsy numbness pains
  My sense, as though of hemlock I had drunk,
Or emptied some dull opiate to the drains
  One minute past, and Lethe-wards had sunk:
'Tis not through envy of thy happy lot,
  But being too happy in thine happiness, —
    That thou, light-winged Dryad of the trees,
      In some melodious plot
  Of beechen green, and shadows numberless,
    Singest of summer in full-throated ease.

II

O, for a draught of vintage! that hath been
  Cool'd a long age in the deep-delved earth,
Tasting of Flora and the country green,
  Dance, and Provençal song, and sunburnt mirth!
O for a beaker full of the warm South,
  Full of the true, the blushful Hippocrene,
    With beaded bubbles winking at the brim,
      And purple-stained mouth;
  That I might drink, and leave the world unseen,
    And with thee fade away into the forest dim:

Fade far away, dissolve, and quite forget
   What thou among the leaves hast never known,
The weariness, the fever, and the fret
   Here, where men sit and hear each other groan;
Where palsy shakes a few, sad, last grey hairs,
    Where youth grows pale, and spectre-thin, and dies;
      Where but to think is to be full of sorrow
        And leaden-eyed despairs,
    Where Beauty cannot keep her lustrous eyes,
     Or new Love pine at them beyond to-morrow.

IV

Away! away! for I will fly to thee,
   Not charioted by Bacchus and his pards,
But on the viewless wings of Poesy,
   Though the dull brain perplexes and retards:
Already with thee! tender is the night,
    And haply the Queen-Moon is on her throne,
      Cluster'd around by all her starry Fays:
        But here there is no light,
    Save what from heaven is with the breezes blown
     Through verdurous glooms and winding mossy ways.

V

I cannot see what flowers are at my feet,
   Nor what soft incense hangs upon the boughs,
But, in embalmed darkness, guess each sweet
   Wherewith the seasonable month endows
The grass, the thicket, and the fruit-tree wild;

White hawthorn, and the pastoral eglantine;
    Fast fading violets cover'd up in leaves;
        And mid-May's eldest child,
The coming musk-rose, full of dewy wine,
    The murmurous haunt of flies on summer eves.

VI

Darkling I listen; and, for many a time
  I have been half in love with easeful Death,
Call'd him soft names in many a mused rhyme,
    To take into the air my quiet breath;
Now more than ever seems it rich to die,
    To cease upon the midnight with no pain,
        While thou art pouring forth thy soul abroad
          In such an ecstasy!
    Still wouldst thou sing, and I have ears in vain —
    To thy high requiem become a sod.

VII

Thou wast not born for death, immortal Bird!
  No hungry generations tread thee down;
The voice I hear this passing night was heard
    In ancient days by emperor and clown:
Perhaps the self-same song that found a path
    Through the sad heart of Ruth, when, sick for home,
        She stood in tears amid the alien corn;
          The same that oft-times hath
    Charm'd magic casements, opening on the foam
    Of perilous seas, in faery lands forlorn.

Forlorn! the very word is like a bell
  To toll me back from thee to my sole self!
Adieu! the fancy cannot cheat so well
  As she is fam'd to do, deceiving elf.
Adieu! adieu! thy plaintive anthem fades
  Past the near meadows, over the still stream,
    Up the hill-side; and now 'tis buried deep
      In the next valley-glades:
  Was it a vision, or a waking dream?
    Fled is that music: — Do I wake or sleep?

And Did Those Feet

William Blake

And did those feet in ancient time
   Walk upon England's mountains green?
And was the holy Lamb of God
   On England's pleasant pastures seen?

And did the Countenance Divine
   Shine forth upon our clouded hills?
And was Jerusalem builded here,
   Among these dark Satanic Mills?

Bring me my bow of burning gold!
   Bring me my arrows of desire!
Bring me my spear! O clouds, unfold!
   Bring me my chariot of fire!

I will not cease from mental fight,
   Nor shall my sword sleep in my hand,
Till we have built Jerusalem
   In England's green and pleasant land.

Daybreak

John Donne

Stay, O sweet, and do not rise!
   The light that shines comes from thine eyes;
The day breaks not: it is my heart,
   Because that you and I must part.
     Stay! or else my joys will die
     And perish in their infancy.

Uriel

Ralph Waldo Emerson

It fell in the ancient periods
    Which the brooding soul surveys,
Or ever the wild Time coined itself
    Into calendar months and days.

This was the lapse of Uriel,
Which in Paradise befell.
Once, among the Pleiads walking,
Seyd overheard the young gods talking;
And the treason, too long pent,
To his ears was evident.
The young deities discussed
Laws of form, and metre just,
Orb, quintessence, and sunbeams,
What subsisteth, and what seems.
One, with low tones that decide,
And doubt and reverend use defied,
With a look that solved the sphere,
And stirred the devils everywhere,
Gave his sentiment divine
Against the being of a line.
'Line in nature is not found;
Unit and universe are round;
In vain produced, all rays return;
Evil will bless, and ice will burn.'
As Uriel spoke with piercing eye,
A shudder ran around the sky;

The stern old war-gods shook their heads,
The seraphs frowned from myrtle-beds;
Seemed to the holy festival
The rash word boded ill to all;
The balance-beam of Fate was bent;
The bounds of good and ill were rent;
Strong Hades could not keep his own,
But all slid to confusion.

A sad self-knowledge, withering, fell
On the beauty of Uriel;
In heaven once eminent, the god
Withdrew, that hour, into his cloud;
Whether doomed to long gyration
In the sea of generation,
Or by knowledge grown too bright
To hit the nerve of feebler sight.
Straightway, a forgetting wind
Stole over the celestial kind,
And their lips the secret kept,
If in ashes the fire-seed slept.
But now and then, truth-speaking things
Shamed the angels' veiling wings;
And, shrilling from the solar course,
Or from fruit of chemic force,
Procession of a soul in matter,
Or the speeding change of water,
Or out of good of evil born,
Came Uriel's voice of cherub scorn,
And a blush tinged the upper sky,
And the gods shook, they knew not why.

PERMISSIONS

"One Art" from *The Complete Poems 1927-1979* by Elizabeth Bishop. Copyright © 1979, 1983 by Alice Helen Methfessel. Reprinted by permission of Farrar, Straus & Giroux, Inc.

Poem 449 from *The Complete Poems of Emily Dickinson by* Emily Dickinson. Copyright 1890, 1891, 1896 by Roberts Brothers. Copyright 1914, 1918, 1919, 1924, 1929, 1930, 1932, 1935, 1937, 1942 by Martha Dickinson Bianchi. Copyright 1951, © 1955 by the President and Fellows of Harvard College. Copyright 1952 by Alfred Leete Hampson. Copyright © 1957, 1958, 1969 by Mary L. Hampson. Published by Little, Brown and Company.

"Bereft" from *The Poetry of Robert Frost,* edited by Edward Connery Lathem. Copyright © 1956 by Robert Frost, copyright 1928, © 1969 by Henry Holt and Company, Inc. Reprinted by permission of Henry Holt and Company, Inc.

"Moriturus" by Edna St. Vincent Millay. From Collected Poems, HarperCollins. Copyright 1928, © 1955 by Edna St. Vincent Millay and Norma Millay Ellis. All rights reserved. Reprinted by per-mission of Elizabeth Barnett, literary executor.

"Arms and the Boy" by Wilfred Owen, from The Collected Poems of Wilfred Owen. Copyright © 1963 by Chatto & Windus, Ltd. Reprinted by permission of New Directions Publishing Corp.

"Coda" by Ezra Pound, from *Personae.* Copyright 1926 by Ezra Pound. Reprinted by permission of New Directions Publishing Corp.

"Fern Hill" by Dylan Thomas, from *The Poems of Dylan Thomas.* Copyright 1945 by The Trustees for the Copyrights of Dylan Thomas. Reprinted by permission of New Directions Publishing Corp.

"Parable" by Richard Wilbur, from *Ceremony and Other Poems,* copyright 1950 and renewed ©1978 by Richard Wilbur. Reprinted by permission of Harcourt Brace & Company.

Index

adjectives: use of, 92
"Ah": use of, 65–66
alexandrine, 33–34, 51
"All for Love" (Byron), 41
alliteration, 57–58
allusion, 74–75
anacrusis, 26–27, 65, 92
anapestic foot (anapest), 7, 13, 16–17, 37, 38–39, 63
"And Did Those Feet" (Blake), 71, 185
"Annabel Lee" (Poe), 38–39, 80, 152–53
Anonymous ("The Wife of Usher's Well"), 32, 47, 147–48
"Arms and the Boy" (Owen), 45, 72, 157
Arnold, Matthew, 47, 163
aspirates, 60
assonance, 57, 58–59
Astrophel and Stella (Sidney), 31, 145

ballad stanza, 32, 51–52
"Bereft" (Frost), 4, 7, 44
Bishop, Elizabeth, 53, 168
Blake, William, 23, 40, 71, 79, 80, 98, 133, 185

blank verse, 48–49
breath, 3–5, 29
breve, 10n
"Bright Star" (Keats), 31, 61, 74, 144
burden, 51
Burns, Robert, 47, 162
Byron, George Gordon, Lord, 17, 36–37, 38, 41, 45, 68, 125–26, 154

caesura, 27, 92
catalectic foot (catalexis), 23, 24, 92
"Chambered Nautilus, The" (Holmes), 43–44, 58, 66, 155–56
Chaucer, Geoffrey, viii
"Coda" (Pound), 8
Coleridge, Samuel Taylor, 55, 59, 80, 173–74
conceit, 72
couplet, 40–45, 52, 91; heroic, 42

dactylic foot (dactyl), 7, 13, 16
dancing: metrical verse and, 87–89
Daniel Deronda (Eliot), 94
"Daybreak" (Donne), 73, 186
"Death of the Hired Man, The" (Frost), 14, 15

"Delight in Disorder" (Herrick), 21, 57, 132
descriptive writing, 98
design, 50–56
"Destruction of Sennacherib, The" (Byron), 17, 68, 125–26
Dickinson, Emily, 32, 45, 79, 149
dimeter, 12
discipline in writing, 94–95
Donne, John, 51, 55, 73, 104, 169–70, 186
double ionic foot, 27, 92

"Eagle, The" (Tennyson), 52, 58, 61, 167
editing poetry, need for, 98–99
eight-foot line. *See* octometer
"Eight O'Clock" (Housman), 48, 164
Eliot, George, 94
Eliot, T. S., 97
Emerson, Ralph Waldo, 46, 65, 75, 79, 93, 158, 187–88
energy release along the line, 36–39
enjambment, 43, 89, 92
"Essay on Criticism, An" (Pope), 34, 42, 81, 150–51
Evangeline (Longfellow), 16
"Eve of St. Agnes, The" (Keats), 54–55
exercise of writing skills, 96–98
exhortations, 65–66
expletives, 65–66

Faerie Queen, The (Spenser), 54
"Farewell! thou art too dear for my possessing" (Shakespeare), 72, 143
feet, 7–18, 19–28; anapestic, 7, 13, 16–17, 37, 38–39, 63; catalectic, 23, 24, 92; dactylic, 7, 13, 16; double ionic, 27, 92; hypersyllabic, 25–26, 80, 92; iambic, 7, 13, 14, 15, 19–21, 22, 24, 33–34, 37, 53, 91; lame, 24, 80; pyrrhic, 27; spondee, 17–18; trochaic, 7, 13, 14–15, 21, 23, 26, 64
feminine rhyme (ending), 21–22, 41, 45
"Fern Hill" (Thomas), 62–63
figurative language, 67–75
five-foot line. *See* pentameter
"Flower, The" (Herbert), 55, 171–72
formal design, 50–56
four-foot line. *See* tetrameter
four-line stanzas (quatrain), 47–48, 55
four-syllable rhyme, 45–46
Frost, Robert, viii, 4–5, 7, 9, 13, 14–15, 18, 21, 31–32, 44, 48, 59, 61, 68, 70, 73, 82, 91, 104, 117–18, 146

"God's Grandeur" (Hopkins), 51, 58, 180

Hamlet (Shakespeare), 19
Hawthorne, Nathaniel, 92
heavy stress, 10n., 10–11
heptameter, 12, 33
Herbert, George, 55, 104, 171–72
heroic couplet, 42
Herrick, Robert, 21, 33, 57, 132
hexameter, 12, 33–34
Holmes, Oliver Wendell, 43–44, 58, 66, 155–56
Hopkins, Gerard Manley, 51, 58, 104, 180
Housman, A. E., 7, 8, 41, 48, 111, 164
hypersyllabic foot, 25–26, 80, 92

iambic foot (iamb), 7, 13, 14, 15, 19–21, 22, 24, 33–34, 37, 53, 91
iambic pentameter, 13, 42, 48–49, 53–55, 91. *See also* iambic foot; pentameter

"I died for Beauty — but was scarce" (Dickinson), 32, 149

image-making, 67–75

imperfect rhyme, 44–45

impure meter, 22, 26

inflection, 8–9; absence of, 9n

In Memoriam (Tennyson), 48, 165

irregularities in meter, 23–25

"I Wander'd Lonely as a Cloud" (Wordsworth), 16, 46, 59, 123

John Keats (Lowell), 95

Keats, John, 20, 30–31, 43, 51, 54, 61, 66, 73, 74, 129, 144, 181–84

"Kubla Khan" (Coleridge), 55, 59, 173–74

lame foot, 24, 80

light stress, 10n., 10–11

line length, 4, 6, 29–35

liquids, 60, 61

Longfellow, Henry Wadsworth, 15, 16, 23, 45, 68, 119–20

"Loveliest of Trees, the Cherry Now" (Housman), 7, 41, 111

Lowell, Amy, 95

Macbeth (Shakespeare), 15, 121–22

macron, 10n

Marlowe, Christopher, 28, 49

Marvell, Andrew, 20, 130–31

masculine rhyme (ending), 22, 41

"Memorial to D.C." (Millay), 59, 64

"Mending Wall" (Frost), 48, 68, 117–18

metaphor, 68–71

metaphysical conceit, 72

meter: non-metric verse and, 62–64

metrical patterns. *See* patterns, metrical

Midsummer Night's Dream, A (Shakespeare), 25, 42, 140

Millay, Edna St. Vincent, 24, 25, 27, 32–33, 51, 59, 63–64, 134–39

Milton, John, viii, 27, 30, 49, 51, 68–70, 141

modesty in writing, 99

monometer, 12

"Moriturus" (Millay), 24, 25, 27, 32–33, 134–39

multisyllabic rhyme, 46

mutes, 60–61

"Naming of Parts" (Reed), 63

octameter, 12, 33, 34

octave, 50–51

"Ode to a Nightingale" (Keats), 66, 181–84

"Ode to the West Wind" (Shelley), 46, 52–53, 159–61

off rhyme, 44–45

"Oh": use of, 65–66

"One Art" (Bishop), 53, 168

one-foot line. *See* monometer

onomatopoeia, 59

"On the Grasshopper and the Cricket" (Keats), 129

Owen, Wilfred, viii, 45, 72, 157

"Ozymandias" (Shelley), 28, 59, 142

"Parable" (Wilbur), 57, 179

Paradise Lost (Milton), 27, 49, 68–70, 141

patterns, metrical, 4, 6–28. *See also* feet; non-metric verse and, 62–64; reading, 87–89

pentameter, 11, 12, 13, 30–31, 35. *See also* iambic pentameter
perfect rhyme, 40
personification, 71–72
Petrarch, 50
Petrarchan conceit, 72
Petrarchan sonnet, 50
physical world: description of, 73–74
playing with technique, 97
Poe, Edgar Allan, 34, 38–39, 45, 79–80, 152–53
Pope, Alexander, 33–34, 42, 79, 81, 150–51
Pound, Ezra, 8
Prelude, The (Wordsworth), 49
pure meter, 22, 26
pyrrhic foot, 27

quatrain, 47–48, 55, 91

"Raven, The" (Poe), 34, 45
"Red, Red Rose, A" (Burns), 47, 162
Reed, Henry, 63
refrain (burden), 51
"Requiem" (Stevenson), 116
"Requiescat" (Arnold), 47, 163
revision of writing, 95–96
"Rhodora, The" (Emerson), 46, 65, 158
rhyme, 4–5, 6, 40–49; couplets, 40–45; four-syllable, 45–46; multisyllable, 46; slant (off; imperfect), 44–45; of sonnet, 50–51; triple, 45; true (perfect), 40
rhythm, 8
Richard III (Shakespeare), 19
"Rime of the Ancient Mariner, The" (Coleridge), 80
Romeo and Juliet (Shakespeare), 51, 166

scansion, 10, 87–92; reading and, 87–89; writing and, 90–92
self-enclosed line, 42
semivowels, 60
sense: pattern and, 9
sestet, 50–51
seven-foot line. *See* heptameter
Shakespeare, William, viii, ix, 14, 18, 19–20, 25, 26, 30, 42, 49, 50–51, 72, 73, 104, 121–22, 127, 128, 140, 143, 166; Sonnet 18, 18, 72, 127; Sonnet 29, 20, 128; Sonnet 87, 72, 143
Shakespearean sonnet, 50–51
"Shall I compare thee to a summer's day?" (Shakespeare), 18, 72, 127
Shelley, Percy Bysshe, 28, 46, 51, 52–53, 55–56, 59, 72, 81, 142, 159–61, 175–78
Sidney, Sir Philip, 31, 51, 145
silences, 60–61
simile, 68–71
six-foot line. *See* alexandrine; hexameter
slant (off; imperfect) rhyme, 44–45
"Song" (Donne), 55, 169–70
Song of Hiawatha, The (Longfellow), 15, 23, 45, 68, 119–20
sonnet, 50; Petrarchan, 50; Shakespearean, 50–51
"So, We'll Go No More A-Roving" (Byron), 36–37
speech-giving, 87–88
Spenser, Edmund, 30, 53–54
Spenserian stanza, 53–54
spondee foot, 17–18
stanzas, 46–47; four-line, 47; variations in pattern of, 80–81
"Stanzas Written on the Road Between Florence and Pisa" (Byron), 154

Stevenson, Robert Louis, 116
"Stopping by Woods on a Snowy Evening" (Frost), 31–32, 59, 70, 91, 146
stress: heavy, 10n, 10–11; light, 10n, 10–11
style, 79–83
substitutions in meter, 13–14
syllabic stresses, 10–11

tag scanning, 22
Tennyson, Alfred Lord, 48, 52, 58, 61, 165, 167
tercets, 52
terza rima, 52–53
tetrameter, 12, 31–32, 41, 51, 64, 91
"Thing of Beauty, A" from *Endymion* (Keats), 43, 114–15
Thomas, Dylan, 62–63
three-foot line. *See* trimeter
"To a Skylark" (Shelley), 55–56, 72, 81, 175–78
"To His Coy Mistress" (Marvell), 130–31
traditional poetic forms, 50–56
trimeter, 12, 37
triple rhyme, 45
trochaic foot (trochee), 7, 13, 14–15, 21, 23, 26, 64

true (perfect) rhyme, 40
"Tuft of Flowers, The" (Frost), 9, 61, 82, 112–13
Twelfth Night (Shakespeare), 26
two-foot line. *See* dimeter
"Tyger, The" (Blake), 40, 133

"Upon His Departure" (Herrick), 33
"Uriel" (Emerson), 75, 187–88

variations in meter, 7–9, 13, 36–37, 80, 89, 91
villanelle, 53

watery sounds, 61
West-Running Brook (Frost), 4
"When in disgrace with Fortune and men's eyes" (Shakespeare), 20, 128
"Wife of Usher's Well, The" (Anonymous), 32, 47, 147–48
Wilbur, Richard, 57, 179
"Witch of Coös, The" (Frost), 14, 18
Wordsworth, William, viii, 16–17, 18, 20, 21, 30, 46, 49, 51, 59, 67, 71–72, 123, 124
"World Is Too Much With Us, The . . ." (Wordsworth), 17, 18, 67, 124